PRAISE FOR

"*Key Figures in Espionage* is a rollicking ride through some of history's most notorious espionage personalities. Well researched and written, the deep dive in to the Cambridge Five is particularly interesting. This book is great for not only the casual reader or spy fan but also for those who are more well versed in the subjects."

— DOUG PATTESON, FORMER CIA OPERATIONS OFFICER

"When it comes to research into the clandestine depths of spycraft, the dynamic duo of Bayard & Holmes have put together a must-read series that is written with authority, yet easily digestible. I've already added their books to my shelf of writing essentials—you should, too!"

— JAMES ROLLINS, #1 NEW YORK TIMES BESTSELLER OF *CRUCIBLE*

ABOUT THE AUTHORS

Piper Bayard is an author and a recovering attorney. She is also a belly dancer, a mom, and a former hospice volunteer. She currently pens spy thrillers with Jay Holmes, as well as her own post-apocalyptic science fiction.

Jay Holmes is a forty-five year veteran of field intelligence operations spanning from the Cold War fight against the Soviets, the East Germans, and the terrorist organizations they sponsored to the present Global War on Terror. Piper is the public face of their partnership.

Together, Bayard & Holmes author nonfiction articles and books on espionage and foreign affairs, as well as fictional spy thrillers. They are the bestselling authors of *The Spy Bride* from the Risky Brides Bestsellers Collection and *Spycraft: Essentials*.

When they aren't writing or, in Jay's case, busy with "other work," Piper and Jay are enjoying their families, hiking, exploring, talking foreign affairs, laughing at their own rude jokes, and questing for the perfect chocolate cake recipe. If you think you have that recipe, please share it with them at their email below.

To receive notices of upcoming Bayard & Holmes releases, subscribe to the Bayard & Holmes Covert Briefing. You can contact Bayard & Holmes at their website BayardandHolmes.com, at @piperbayard on Twitter, or at their email, BayardandHolmes@protonmail.com.

ALSO BY BAYARD & HOLMES

AVAILABLE AT BAYARDANDHOLMES.COM

———

NONFICTION

Spycraft: Essentials

Key Moments in Espionage

Timeline Iran: Stone Age to Nuclear Age

———

COMING SOON

Key People and Wars

———

FICTION BY BAYARD & HOLMES

The Spy Bride

Apex Predator Series Coming Soon

The Panther of Baracoa

The Leopard of Cairo

The Caiman of Iquitos

———

FICTION BY PIPER BAYARD

Firelands

KEY FIGURES IN ESPIONAGE

THE GOOD, THE BAD, & THE BOOTY

BAYARD & HOLMES

SPYCRAFT II

Shoe Phone Press
2770 Arapahoe Road #132-229
Lafayette, CO 80026

Copyright © 2019 by Bayard & Holmes

All rights reserved as permitted under the U.S. Copyright Act of 1976. No portion
of this publication may be reproduced in any form or by any electronic or
mechanical means, including information storage and retrieval systems,
without written permission from the authors, with the exception of reviewers,
who may quote brief passages in a book review.

To all of those with stars on the Wall,

and to all who have earned them,

but will never be known to have done so.

CONTENTS

INTRODUCTION

In our first Spycraft Series book, *Spycraft: Essentials*, we explored the jurisdictions and duties of the main civilian intelligence organizations, terminology, recruitment, basic tradecraft, espionage myths, firearms, and the personalities and personal challenges of those brave souls who populate the US Intelligence Community ("IC"). That book is more of a what's happening and a how-to, including tips for authors to help them get some of the fiction out of their fiction. In this book, we shift focus to take a closer look at some of the figures in espionage who have quietly influenced the course of history—some for good, some for bad, and some by using the gifts their mamas gave them.

We have only one overarching writing tip: Study the very real people you will find in these pages, because nothing in fiction can compare to the courage of these heroes, or to the depravity of the villains they must overcome.

We all like to think of history as being set in stone—something solid that we can stand on to guide us when the storm clouds gather, and something to remind us that no matter how bad things get, someone has faced it before, and someone has survived it before. However, when we dig past the clickbait and agendas of the past, we find that what seem to be solid facts are actually fragments of truth laced together in a spider web of inaccurate guesses, honest misunderstandings, deliberate misrepresentations, and the outright lies of the winners. Nevertheless, we are stuck with the paradox that if we don't make sense of history, we can never make sense of the now.

We are all caught in a perpetual loop of the movie Groundhog Day. On a global scale, each generation is born with the same challenges, desires, shortcomings, and hubris, and nothing is happening on the planet that hasn't been happening since the caveman days of Ogg and Uga. Each generation learns the same lessons and wrings its hands in frustration as the next generation ignores its warnings. Therefore, when we study the triumphs and betrayals of the past, we are seeking out the clues past generations have left for us in the hope of understanding the present.

Countries, governments, and technologies can change rapidly. But people? People, as a collective, change at a glacial pace if at all. Sure, views and habits come in and out of fashion, but basic motivations of humanity remain the same. Therefore, one of the best ways to gain insight into people and societies of today is to study history and the individuals who created it. By doing so, we find that many heroes are simply common people called to greatness by their circumstances. We find that some who are now called heroes were really only pawns. And we find that still others who could have been heroes chose instead to be instruments of treachery. Through the character, motives, courage, egos, and decadence of individuals throughout history, we are informed on the heights and depths of human nature, which is at the heart of every government and every endeavor. Studying the individuals of the past gives us insight into what moves the geopolitical tides in our world today, as well as where that flow is taking us tomorrow.

While this is true in every field, *Key Figures in Espionage* focuses on individuals in the arena of the Shadow World—that underground current of humanity that pulses between countries and epochs, quietly carrying out the background work of nations. We focus on a few good guys, a few bad guys, and a few booty spies to illuminate the courage and depravity that humans possess, some devoting their lives to service, and some killing with impunity to gratify their own egos.

Honeypots and booty spies are pretty clear, but what constitutes the "good" and the "bad" depends on where a person sits. So where do we sit?

We are unapologetically American in our value judgments on these matters. Piper is an author and a recovering attorney who has worked daily with Holmes for the past decade, learning about foreign affairs, espionage history, and field techniques for the purpose of writing both fiction and nonfiction. Holmes is a forty-five-year veteran of field espionage operations. Since Holmes is still covert, Piper is the public face of their partnership.

The style of this book is narrative nonfiction. We researched the biographies contained in this book through open sources and only included information that is verifiable in the public forum. Also, as noted above, much of history is shrouded in inaccuracies. Therefore, we have noted discrepancies and verified the information included through more than one open source that we consider to be reliable.

Espionage buffs might be asking where we hid the chapter about the Walker family spy ring. We didn't forget those dirtbags. We cover them thoroughly in *Spycraft: Essentials*, so we don't think it's right to repeat ourselves and sell it to readers twice. The same is true of the US Navy/Fat Leonard Conspiracy, which is also covered in *Spycraft: Essentials*.

Come with us now, and as we wade through the echoes of the past that we so confidently refer to as "history," while keeping in mind that there is no such thing as history. It's all continuing to unfold. There are still many who are noble and brave; there are still many who can strip a gear in the sanest mind with their treachery; there are still many who would surrender their nation for a subtle caress or a compassionate ear. When we learn about the past, we learn about today.

THE GOOD

Lydia Darragh
An Inconspicuous Quaker Woman

Moe Berg
Pro Baseball Player, Lawyer, Linguist, Operative

Virginia Hall
The Most Dangerous Spy in All of France

Jozef Gabčík & Jan Kubiš
Assassins of Reinhard Heydrich

Eric Roberts
The "Untalented" Bank Clerk

Ian Fleming
The Man Who Wrote the Myth

Billy Waugh
Perseverance Personified

Fernando "X"
El Tigre Con Cojones Immensos

Analysts
The Heroes Who Will Never Be in Movies

1

LYDIA DARRAGH

AN INCONSPICUOUS QUAKER WOMAN

IN REAL LIFE, VERSUS HOLLYWOOD, NOT ALL INTELLIGENCE personnel are highly-trained supermen and superwomen who look like Daniel Craig and Scarlett Johansson. Many are simple people who rise to the occasion of their moment in history. Lydia Darragh was one of those people—a common woman in uncommon circumstances. She never set out to be a spy, and she was never trained or equipped for the work, but when history called on her to be an asset for General George Washington, she stepped up.

On a chilly rainy day in Dublin in 1729, a baby girl was born in front of a quaint Irish stone hearth in a humble home. . . . Well, okay, we can't be sure of the rain, but if you've been to Dublin, you can imagine a little rain falling. The house was likely humble, and why not get close to the fireplace if you have to give birth in Dublin in 1729?

What we do know for certain is that the girl was named Lydia Barrington, and at the age of twenty-four, she married a clergyman's son named William Darragh. Two years later, they weathered the hazardous crossing to the British colonies in America and settled in Philadelphia.

Lydia and William were pacifists and joined a Quaker community. Lydia, a nurse and midwife, was evidently a durable woman, as she gave birth to nine children and managed not to die in the process. The Darraghs lost four children in infancy and raised their five surviving children to be practicing Quakers. However, during the American Revolution, their son Charles defied his upbringing and joined the Second Pennsylvania Regiment to fight against the British occupation.

On September 26, 1777, British forces led by General Howe entered Philadelphia in force. Howe occupied the home of Lydia's neighbor, John Cadwalader, who was absent, having joined the revolutionary regiment known as The Light Horse of the City of Philadelphia, a.k.a. the Philadelphia Light Horse. As was common practice at the time, Howe stationed soldiers in the homes of the local citizens. Upon arriving at his new headquarters, Howe dispatched his intelligence officer, Major John Andre, to commandeer more houses for his staff officers and their attendants. Major Andre ordered Lydia and her family to move out of their home.

Lydia and William had two young children still at home and no place to go, so Lydia decided to ask Lord Howe to allow her to stay in her home. On her way to Howe's headquarters at Cadwalader's, she met up with a cousin from Ireland, who happened to be a captain on Howe's staff. Her cousin interceded for her, and Howe allowed Lydia and her children to remain in their home with the understanding that she would keep her dining room available as a meeting room for British officers.

On the night of December 2, 1777, Howe held a planning session with his senior staff members and his unit commanders at the Darragh residence. They worked for several hours to formalize the details of an attack on the Revolutionary Forces stronghold of Whitemarsh, to be conducted on December 4. During this planning session, Lydia hid in a linen closet next to the meeting room. Had she been discovered, she likely would have been taken outside and hanged as a spy. However, she was perhaps emboldened by the knowledge that her son Charles's regiment was at Whitemarsh with General Washington, and she took the risk.

As the meeting broke up, Lydia quickly snuck back to bed. Major Andre knocked on her door, but she ignored him the first few times. Finally, she answered, and Andre told her that the meeting was over. Lydia knew that she had two days to alert Washington's forces of the pending British attack. The next day, Lydia requested a pass to get flour at a mill in the countryside. Locals frequently requested such passes to purchase supplies from nearby farming communities.

The remainder of Lydia's story is somewhat controversial. According to her daughter Ann, she found Thomas Craig, a member of the Pennsylvania militia, at the Rising Sun tavern, and he relayed Lydia's information to Washington. In another version handed down from Colonel Elias Boudinot's family, Colonel Boudinot was dining at the Rising Sun tavern when Lydia approached him and passed him a note hidden in a small sewing kit. In that version, it was Boudinot who alerted Washington to the pending attack. It may be that Lydia was simply being a good intelligence agent and chose not to rely upon only one person to deliver the critical message to Washington. Therefore, we suspect that both accounts are true.

What is certain is that Washington did, indeed, get the message, and it's a good thing that he did. He was considering moving the greater part of his forces further north. Many of his nine thousand troops were recently-arrived reinforcements from New York and Maryland. They were ill-equipped, inexperienced, and road weary. Had Howe and his ten thousand experienced, well-equipped troops caught up to Washington, they would likely have destroyed the better part of the Colonial forces. With the new information in hand, Washington and his staff were able to prepare to resist an attack.

Just after midnight on December 5, General Cornwallis led the British vanguard into an ambush by Captain Allan McLane's Colonial cavalry patrol. Captain McLane dispatched riders to alert nearby pickets. When he and his force withdrew, the arrogant Cornwallis was certain that he had won the skirmish. He failed to understand what was occurring. McLane had simply wanted to make contact with the British forces in order to determine their arrival time.

Over the following two days, the British easily held off limited American advances. Cornwallis was deceived, but Howe was not. Howe was a brilliant soldier and understood the Americans better than most of his contemporaries did. He knew Washington was merely keeping track of British dispositions so as to better organize to meet a British attack on the prepared Colonial defensive positions.

Howe expected to fight for a maximum of two days to destroy the Colonial Army. Hoping to surprise Washington in the open, he had ordered that his army's heavy baggage be left behind in Philadelphia. His troops had now slept in the open for two days and were short on rations.

To Cornwallis's surprise, and to the considerable disappointment of Washington and his staff, Howe ordered a withdrawal to Philadelphia. Cornwallis and others later criticized him for this move, but had his hungry, tired men attacked the Colonials, the long range fire of the Colonials' rifles would likely have taken a huge toll on Howe's forces before they could even get close to the enemy lines.

It was obvious to Howe that Washington had been warned of the British attack. The British questioned everyone in the area, but fortunately for Lydia, they settled on the theory that a trained spy from Washington's camp must have guessed at their preparations to march and relayed a message using the usual American relay rider tactic.

Given Lydia's connection to a member of Howe's staff, it's easy to see how even a bright man like Howe might have assumed that the Quaker woman was a British loyalist. She hailed from an English Irish family in Dublin, and Quakers of all backgrounds were seen as being often-annoying, but never dangerous. In Lydia's case, the reasonable assumptions turned out to be bad assumptions.

Some historians interpret Lydia's story as proof that General Howe and his army thought too little of women to think them capable of spying. This seems unlikely. Howe's trusted intelligence officer Major Andre was not in the habit of underestimating women and often employed women as spies for the British. Lydia simply played her role as a friendly sympathizer well.

In overall casualties, the Battle of Whitemarsh was insignificant, but strategically, it was important for the American rebels. It allowed Washington to safely withdraw his forces to Valley Forge, where they faced a bitter winter, but they were able to survive and renew their offensive in the spring. Without the advanced, detailed warning that the old Quaker pacifist gave, Washington's army might have never made it as far as Valley Forge.

And what became of Lydia Darragh? She remained in Philadelphia long after the British were gone. Her husband William passed on in 1783, and in 1786, Lydia moved from their home to finish out her days as a storekeeper. She died in 1789.

Lydia Darragh was an inconspicuous Quaker woman that circumstance called to duty. In truth, if the stories of all the individuals who have helped American and allied causes were known, we would quickly see that few are highly-trained James Bond types. Intelligence personnel come in all sizes and shapes, and from a plethora of backgrounds and situations. What Lydia Darragh proved is that rather than training, privilege, or skill, it is often heart and the commitment to one's cause that matter the most.

2

MOE BERG

PRO BASEBALL PLAYER, LAWYER, LINGUIST, OPERATIVE

RENAISSANCE MAN MOE BERG EXEMPLIFIES A QUINTESSENTIAL combination of intelligence and devotion. Quiet and unassuming, he proved time and again that he had no interest in the fame or fortune that could have been his, but that instead, he was solely dedicated to the mission. Like so many in the Intelligence Community, he was a brilliant and devoted professional who served throughout his life with no real recognition or appreciation, but who made an indelible mark on history.

On March 2, 1902, an unremarkable Jewish immigrant couple in upper Manhattan had their day brightened by the birth of a healthy baby boy. They named him Morris Berg. Little did they know that Morris would grow up to be a professional baseball player, a Columbia law graduate, and a WWII spy against the Japanese.

Morris's father was a pharmacist, and he and his wife were more educated than the average immigrant. They read to Morris and taught him counting and basic math skills at an early age. Before he turned four, Morris begged his parents to enter him in school.

He was too young to attend, but his education at home picked up pace.

The Morris family moved to a middle class neighborhood in West Newark, New Jersey in 1910. There, Morris learned to hide his Jewish identity in order to register for the local Roseville Methodist Episcopal Church Baseball League. Those who played baseball with Morris remembered him as being a great player and an even better person. He was universally appreciated on the teams he played on through his childhood. His schoolmates liked him because, in spite of his brilliance at academics, he was able to fit in with any group of kids. His teachers remembered him as a leader and a peacemaker on the playground.

Morris attended New York University in 1919 and transferred to Princeton the following year. He was the star of the Princeton baseball team and graduated Magna Cum Laude after passing language tests in seven foreign languages: English, Latin, Greek, Hebrew, French, Spanish, and German.

One might think a Princeton graduate who spoke seven languages would go straight into academics, banking, or the State Department. But why do that when he could be a professional baseball player? In 1923, Morris "Moe" Berg landed a gig as a short stop and utility infielder for the Brooklyn Robins, the precursor to the Brooklyn Dodgers. Even with a career in baseball, Moe continued his education, traveling to Paris during his winter vacations from baseball to study Japanese, Chinese, Korean, Arabic, Sanskrit, and Hungarian at La Sorbonne.

Then Moe, not content with playing professional baseball in the warm months and studying languages in the winter, enrolled in Columbia University Law School. He also joined the Chicago White Sox roster as a short stop in 1925, but reported late in order to finish his first year at Columbia Law. During his tenure with the White Sox, the team ran out of catchers due to injuries. Moe filled in. When he proved to be a better catcher than he was a short stop, he became a permanent catcher.

Due to his baseball career, Moe was unable to attend his law classes in a normal sequence. As a result, he grew impatient, and sat for the infamously difficult New York State bar exam before graduating from law school. He passed the bar and later received his law degree from Columbia University.

In 1932, Japan requested that Major League Baseball send a coaching staff of pitchers and at least one catcher to teach as roving coaches at Japan's major universities. Lefty O'Doul, Ted Lyons, and other top players answered the call and went to Japan. Oddly, mediocre catcher Moe Berg accompanied them.

What Moe lacked in hitting skills, he more than made up for in social skills, and he befriended many influential Japanese professors and business people that winter in Japan. As spring training approached, the other players returned directly to the United States. Moe, however, received permission to travel to Japanese-occupied Manchuria, and then to return home via stops in Peking, Shanghai, Siam, India, Cairo, and Berlin. Though he was keeping his eyes open in all of those countries, Japan was the critical part of the trip and the target of his attentions, as that country was still quite closed.

Two years later, Japan requested that Major League Baseball send an All Star team to tour Japan and show off their skills to young Japanese players. The All Star roster was set, and it naturally did not include the average professional catcher Moe Berg. However, at the last moment, and to the amusement of the All Stars, Moe was added to the roster and made the trip. He delivered the welcoming ceremony speech for the All Stars in fluent Japanese. The Japanese were so delighted they invited Moe to address the Japanese legislature, where he also gave a charming speech.

On November 29, 1934, while his team was playing in Omiya, the team manager excused Moe from the game to visit the daughter of the US Ambassador, who was in Saint Luke's Hospital in Tokyo. At the hospital, Berg sneaked onto the locked roof and filmed the Tokyo skyline, including shipyard areas and new cranes at Japanese shipbuilding facilities that were of particular concern to the US Navy.

In our age of satellites and drones, it might seem like a minor accomplishment, but we should remember that Japan had closed its ports to foreigners, and few foreigners were allowed to travel there. From the photographs Moe took, the US Navy deduced that Japan had, indeed, broken the London Naval Agreement of 1930 and was building heavier battleships than the agreement had allowed. The cranes in Moe's photos were larger and more expensive than what was required to build even Japan's heaviest ships allowed under the agreement. Eight years later in 1942, Berg's films of Tokyo were still highly relevant, and they were instrumental in planning the bombing mission for the daring Tokyo Bombing Raid launched from a carrier group commanded by Admiral Halsey and led by US Army Colonel James Doolittle.

When the United States entered WWII after the Japanese raid on Pearl Harbor on December 7, 1941, Moe accepted a position with the Office of Inter-American Affairs. His position was officially that of a health inspector for US troops in the Caribbean and South America, but he was, in fact, operating in a counterintelligence role. He found the work boring.

Two years later, Moe volunteered for work in German-occupied territory with the Office of Strategic Services ("OSS"). It was during this phase of his life that Moe Berg provided his greatest service to the United States and her allies.

Berg's first major success came in the fall of 1943, when he parachuted into Nazi-occupied Yugoslavia and rendezvoused with the two major resistance groups. He evaluated both groups in terms of strength and leadership and delivered a report to the OSS, which helped the United States decide to support the Tito-led partisans as the most viable anti-Nazi resistance fighters. The United States provided Tito's fighters with the supplies and equipment they needed to confront the Germans, forcing the Nazis to keep supplies and several extra divisions in Yugoslavia when they instead might have been used effectively in offensive operations against the Soviet Army.

After his work in Yugoslavia, Berg led a team of agents on kidnapping missions in Italy, where they were able to snatch important Italian scientists and assist others in escaping to the West. The secret mission within that mission that only Berg was told about was to find out from the Italians what German physicists Werner Heisenberg and Carl Friedrich Von Weizsäcker might be doing concerning the development of an atomic weapon.

Berg reported that Heisenberg, the leader of the Nazi Atomic Bomb project, was going to deliver a lecture in Zurich. Moe used his social skills to finagle an invitation to the lecture and to the dinner in Heisenberg's honor.

The OSS ordered Berg to evaluate Heisenberg. If it seemed to him that Heisenberg was on the right track, specifically gas fusion separation of Uranium isotopes instead of the dead-end heavy water method of acquiring the proper isotope for making a nuclear weapon, then Moe was to "honor" Heisenberg by emptying a magazine of .32 caliber ammunition into the man's head and chest and rendezvous with an escape team. Just as importantly, if Heisenberg did not seem to be up to the job, Berg was to leave him alive so as to avoid having the German Atomic Bomb project placed under the leadership of the more-brilliant and capable Carl Weizsäcker.

From the lectures and the dinner conversation, Berg determined that Heisenberg was, indeed, as overrated as escaped German scientists had claimed he was, and that Heisenberg lacked the brilliance in theoretical physics and mathematics necessary to make decisions about the project. Berg decided not to kill Heisenberg. The average professional baseball catcher had been able to see through Heisenberg's pro-Nazi, bloated reputation and left him in charge of the Nazi atom bomb efforts.

Other aspects of Berg's work in Europe in WWII remain classified. However, it is believed by some that he was responsible for establishing an effective channel of communication between the German scientific community and the US government, and that this channel paid dividends concerning a multitude of German research and weapons development efforts.

On October 10, 1945, President Truman, with the approval of the US Congress, awarded Moe Berg the nation's highest civilian award, the Medal of Freedom. According to Central Intelligence Agency ("CIA") sources, Berg felt that the work that he and his team had done would remain important due to a Soviet threat that many had not yet perceived. He respectfully declined the medal and asked that the matter remain quiet for the sake of the mission.

Berg's life remains something of a mystery from 1945 to 1951. However, in 1951, he was back "on the books" with the CIA as a contractor. He requested that he be sent to Israel, but he was instead ordered back to Europe to recruit agents for the young intelligence agency.

Moe Berg had been a fabulously successful special operations officer, but the CIA mysteriously failed to notice his lack of training for recruiting agents from peace-time Europe. The agency apparently assumed that Moe would use his brilliance to work out the details for himself.

While Berg might, in fact, have been able to recruit agents, he would *not*, as a contract agent, have been practically able to insert himself into the role of senior agent recruiter and handler for US teams working in Europe. These teams would never have accepted an outsider into their niche without him or her having been brought through the normal training and acclimation that the European teams had gone through at the time. With no support from the CIA European Station Teams and no special channels set up for him by the agency, Berg's mission was something less than a success. In 1953, the CIA declined to renew Moe's contract.

Berg spent the next eighteen years of his life in seeming apathy and unemployment. There are rumors that during this period, he worked with contacts from within East Germany and the Balkans as part of an "old boy network" outside of the Western intelligence structure to obtain intelligence on the Soviet Union's scientific efforts. These rumors cannot be confirmed.

Moe Berg died on May 29, 1972, of natural causes. The US government requested that his sister accept on his behalf what Moe had refused in life—the Medal of Freedom. She accepted.

Though Berg made countless important contributions to the US Intelligence Community, perhaps his most enduring was in helping the IC learn that it is extremely difficult for employee station teams that are working under diplomatic cover to support deniable contract agents and their assets with communications and logistics. That knowledge came too late to make proper use of Moe Berg's remarkable talents during the early 1950s, but thankfully, that particular mistake has not been repeated in later years.

3

VIRGINIA HALL

THE MOST DANGEROUS SPY IN ALL OF FRANCE

SAY THE NAME "VIRGINIA HALL" TO ANYONE IN THE CLANDESTINE Services, and they may well get choked up with reverence. We certainly do. Being a woman with no special physical ability and lacking one leg, no recruiter then or now would entertain thoughts of Virginia being capable of military service—especially behind enemy lines. Nevertheless, she was determined to serve an active role in the battle against Nazi Germany, and serve she did, becoming one of the most revered 20th century icons in the Intelligence Community. Altogether remarkable, she is a breathtaking example of selflessness, courage, and commitment.

Virginia Hall was born on April 6, 1906, to a wealthy family in Baltimore, Maryland. Having a gift for languages, she studied French, German, and Italian at Radcliffe College and Barnard College and then traveled to Europe to continue her education in Austria, France, and Germany. Virginia hoped that her language skills would allow her to enter the US Foreign Service.

After finishing her studies in 1931, she was hired as a Consular Service clerk at the US Embassy in Warsaw. From there, she was assigned to a consulate office in Izmir, Turkey. While in Turkey,

Virginia had a hunting accident and had to have her lower left leg amputated. She obtained a wooden prosthetic leg, which she named "Cuthbert," and was then assigned to the US consulate in Venice.

Virginia requested permission to take the US Foreign Service Exam, but she was informed that, due to her injury, she could not apply for a position as a diplomat. She returned to the United States and attended graduate school at American University in Washington, DC.

When Germany invaded France in 1940, Virginia was visiting Paris. She responded to the invasion by volunteering with the French Ambulance Corps and driving ambulances to evacuate wounded French soldiers from the front. When France surrendered to Germany, Virginia escaped to Spain, and then on to England.

In London, Virginia met Vera Atkins, a recruiter for British Special Operations Executive ("SOE"). The circumstances of that fateful meeting are not clear. Some sources say they met on a train while evacuating France, and others claim that they met at a party in London. Never one to avoid danger, Virginia applied for service in the British SOE and was accepted. With the SOE, Virginia trained in weapons, communications, and as a resistance organizer for occupied France, and in August of 1941, she infiltrated Vichy. Some sources state that she was the first female SOE agent to do so.

The United States was not yet directly involved in the war, so Virginia posed as a news correspondent for the New York Post. Once the United States did enter the war in December of 1941, the sensible thing for her to do would have been to hustle back to England. Fortunately for the Allied effort, she declined to escape and went underground.

When Virginia infiltrated Vichy, France in 1941, the Vichy Republic region was not yet occupied by Germany because the Pétain government fully collaborated with the Nazis. At that time, operating in Vichy was more dangerous for an SOE agent than operating in the Nazi-occupied region of France. The Vichy government had command of the French police departments, and with so many reliable local assets, it could more easily discover infiltrators and resistors. Most SOE agents sent into Vichy, France in 1941 and 1942 were killed or captured within days.

Virginia clearly had the right talents, education, courage, and determination for her difficult work. She quickly earned a reputation as a great recruiter and resistance organizer in France. She was instrumental in the rescue of hundreds of downed Allied aviators, and she arranged their safe return to England. She also organized a network of safe houses and coordinated numerous air drops of weapons and supplies to the French Resistance at a time when most drops were being intercepted by the Vichy police and the Gestapo. Virginia's successes did not go completely unnoticed by the Vichy government and the Nazi Gestapo. The Gestapo branded her as the most dangerous spy in all of France, and they made her capture a priority.

In November of 1942, most of the Vichy-controlled French colonial military forces in northwest Africa offered only token resistance to the Allied landings in Morocco, Algeria, and Tunisia. The Nazis decided that the Vichy government was not collaborating to Hitler's satisfaction, and they took over control of the Vichy Republic. Infamous Gestapo leader Klaus Barbie demanded that "the woman with the limp," as Virginia was known, be captured and brought directly to him so that he could personally strangle her.

Virginia used her one good leg to stay one step ahead of the Gestapo, and that November, she escaped on foot over the Pyrenees to Spain. Some convincing sources say she was alone on this trip. Some other convincing sources say she was *not* alone on this trip. It is possible that she made more than one trip over the Pyrenees. This is only one of many uncertainties about Virginia Hall's career, as she knew all too well that spies who don't take their secrets to the grave can end up in the grave all too soon.

One thing all sources agree on is that during the November 1942 trek over the snow-covered mountains, Virginia radioed her progress to the SOE and mentioned that she hoped that "Cuthbert" would not give her too much trouble. The SOE officer that responded, apparently not in on the joke, messaged back that if Cuthbert gave her trouble, he should be "eliminated." Fortunately, Virginia managed to keep Cuthbert in her service and made it to Spain.

However, she had no identification papers at a time when such documents were crucial. She was arrested by the Spanish and incarcerated for several weeks. When the US consulate in Barcelona learned of this, they claimed Virginia as a legitimate US citizen and demanded her release.

Virginia then began working undercover in Spain. After four months, she decided that she was no longer achieving enough on behalf of the war effort, and she returned to England in 1943 in the hope of doing more "useful" work.

Back in England, King George VI presented her with an Honorary Membership in the Order of the British Empire for her remarkable courage and successes. Though she could have accepted a position as an instructor or agent handler in the United Kingdom, Virginia left the SOE to join the fledgling American OSS. Remarkably, she volunteered to return to occupied France.

Virginia dyed her hair gray and disguised herself as an elderly farmer. Since her wooden leg made a nighttime parachute drop too dangerous for her, she was infiltrated back to Bretagne, France on a British torpedo boat. Using the alias "Marcelle Montagne" and the code name "Diane," one of the many code names she used over the years, she made her way to central France, where she set up radio communications with London. In addition to transmitting intelligence back to London, Virginia again organized successful supply drops for the French Resistance, established safe houses, helped train three battalions of Free French guerrilla forces, and linked up with a Jedburgh team after the Allied invasion. In spite of Klaus Barbie's personal vendetta against her, Virginia avoided capture and continued operating until the Allies liberated central France in 1944.

In September of 1945, on behalf of a grateful nation, OSS General William "Wild Bill" Donovan presented Virginia Hall with a Distinguished Service Cross. That was the highest honor received by any female civilian during WWII. President Truman had intended to present her the award in a public ceremony at the White House, but Virginia insisted that the ceremony be kept from public view because she was "anxious to get back to work" and still needed her cover. She wasn't finished yet.

Virginia went to work undercover in Italy operating against Soviet efforts to cultivate Italian communist groups. Afterward, she worked with a CIA front group, the National Committee for a Free Europe, which was associated with Radio Free Europe.

In 1950, Virginia married OSS Agent Paul Goillot, and in the following year, both Virginia and her husband joined the newly-established CIA. Virginia became an expert on resistance groups in Soviet-occupied Europe, remaining in the shadows and working on a variety of projects until her retirement in 1966.

Virginia Hall Goillot passed away of natural causes at Shady Grove Adventist Hospital in Rockville, Maryland, on July 8, 1982.

To this day, her remarkable history of selfless service in the cause of freedom remains a brilliant example for the intrepid few who might dare to follow in her footsteps.

4

JOZEF GABČÍK & JAN KUBIŠ

OPERATION ANTHROPOID—THE ASSASSINATION OF
REINHARD HEYDRICH

THE BUTCHER OF PRAGUE . . . THE BLOND BEAST . . . THE
Hangman. These were names whispered with terror that all
meant only one man—Nazi SS-Obergruppenführer Reinhard
Heydrich. His entire résumé of ruthless deeds is too long for this
book, but notably, he concocted the idea of the Einsatzgruppen,
a.k.a. the death squads of the SS. Their primary mission was to
eliminate all sources of resistance to German domination by
killing all "undesirable" people, including Jews, Slavs, Polish
intelligentsia, communists, Roma ("Gypsies"), homosexuals, and
the disabled. He is the man who outlined what is known today as
the Holocaust.

In 1941, Heydrich was appointed the governor of the Nazi-occupied territory between Germany and Russia. He ran his pseudo
kingdom from Prague, where he quickly earned his monikers by
executing three hundred Czechs and imprisoning thousands
more within the first five weeks.

Enter Jozef Gabčík and Jan Kubiš, two regular paratroopers who
became immortal in the world of espionage by pulling off one of
the most daring and consequential feats in history—the assassi-

nation of Reinhard Heydrich. They did not accomplish this feat with a perfect plan that was perfectly executed, but rather they succeeded after everything had gone completely wrong. An analysis of their circumstances two days before the assassination would lead any normal person to conclude the mission was blown and no longer worth pursuing. Jozef Gabčík and Jan Kubiš did it anyway.

When the Nazis invaded the area that was known as Czechoslovakia, they devoted themselves to destroying the history of the area. Anything they missed was largely obliterated by the Soviets who came in on their heels. As a result, it is difficult to find information on individuals in that region. However, this is what we do know of these two espionage icons.

Jozef Gabčík was born on April 8, 1912, in Rajecfürdő, Austria-Hungary, an area that was known as Czechoslovakia from the end of WWI until the fall of the Soviet Union, and which is in Slovakia today. As a boy, Jozef had a reputation for being an extremely hard worker both in school and at home. In his youth, he took up residence with a farrier, a.k.a. a horse shoer, to learn that trade, as well as blacksmithing.

Apparently, that wasn't enough to keep such an industrious young man busy. Jozef also studied to be a clockmaker, and in 1927, he enrolled in business school. Then, still prior to WWII, Jozef joined the Czech Army and rose to the equivalent rank of a US Army Staff Sergeant. After the Nazi invasion of Czechoslovakia, he traveled to France to fight the Germans during the invasion of that country. When France fell, Jozef made it to the United Kingdom and joined other Czech fighters that organized there as the Free Czech Army, headquartered in Cholmondeley Castle in Cheshire. It was there that Jozef met his partner in fate, Jan Kubiš.

Jan Kubiš was born on June 24, 1913, in Dolní Vilémovice in Austria-Hungary, which is today part of the Czech Republic. Jan was known to be outgoing and sociable and had a reputation for being popular with the ladies. He was an outdoor enthusiast and became an avid Boy Scout. He also joined the Orel Athletic Group, which was a Catholic-sponsored national athletic movement.

In November of 1935, Jan joined the Czech Army and rose to the equivalent rank of a US Army Platoon Sergeant. After the German invasion of Czechoslovakia in March of 1939, Jan went to Poland, where many Czech refugees organized to fight the Germans. After Poland fell to the Nazis, he joined the French Foreign Legion and fought the Germans in France. Then, when France fell, Jan went to the United Kingdom to Cholmondeley Castle to join the Free Czech Army and keep fighting.

In the Czechoslovakian infantry brigade, Jozef served as a mechanic, and Jan served as an electrician. In the United Kingdom, they continued their military service doing parachute training under British instruction. The two men became fast friends.

František Moravec, head of the Czech intelligence services in the United Kingdom, worked with Brigadier Colin Gubbins, who at the time was the Director of Operations in the British Special Operations Executive, to plan the fall of Reinhard Heydrich. Moravec chose two dozen of the two thousand Czech soldiers in exile and sent them to the SOE training centers in Arisaig, Scotland. The mission, dubbed Operation Anthropoid, was originally scheduled for October 28, 1941, but Gabčík's first partner, Staff Sergeant Karel Svoboda, suffered a head injury during training. Jan Kubiš was selected to replace Svoboda. Operation Anthropoid was delayed for Kubiš to complete training and to obtain counterfeit documents.

On December 28, 1941, after extensive training in commando tactics and, for Jan, riding a bicycle, Gabčík, Kubiš, and five other Czech soldiers parachuted into Czechoslovakia with two other groups, Silver A and Silver B, that were on different missions. The seven men had instructions to assassinate Heydrich and escape south to Slovakia.

Before they could do this, they first had to find their way to what was supposed to have been their landing site. The pilots of the two planes had some navigation problems and dropped the paratroopers near Nehvizdy, northeast of Prague—approximately 122 km away from their planned site, which was Plzeň, southwest of Prague. The men first made their way to Plzeň, and from there, they moved on to Prague.

According to some sources, the men were instructed that under no circumstances were they to contact anyone in the Czech Underground. However, the men were undercover in Nazi-occupied territory, tasked with killing a genocidal titan with nothing but guns, a small bomb, and their cyanide pills as a last resort should they fail. They contacted several families and anti-Nazi organizations in Prague.

Over the few months after their insertion behind enemy lines, Gabčík and Kubiš considered numerous plans for assassinating Heydrich. They first intended to get to him on a train, but then realized that was not feasible. Their second plan was to dispatch Heydrich in the forest between his home and Prague. They got so far as to wait several hours in the forest, ready to pull a cable across the road to stop Heydrich's car. However, when there was no sign of Heydrich, their commander, Lt. Adolf Opálka, picked up Gabčík and Kubiš and took them back to Prague. The two men then decided they would kill Heydrich in the city.

Fortunately for Jan and Jozef, as well as for the rest of the world, Heydrich was cocky. Not only did he like to ride in an open car, but he kept the same routine, travelling the same roads on a regular basis in the back of a Mercedes 320 C convertible. After months of moving around and six weeks of hiding out with František Moravec's family in Žižkov, Prague 3, Jan and Jozef took their chance.

Their plan was to kill Heydrich at a sharp curve on the road into Prague. Jozef was to gun the Butcher down with a machine gun when his driver slowed for the curve. Jan stood ready with a small, modified anti-tank grenade in a briefcase should something go wrong. And why would they think anything could go wrong after almost everything had gone wrong already?

On the morning of May 27, 1942, Gabčík and Kubiš waited for Heydrich at a tram stop near St. Nicholas bridge with their fellow, Josef Valčík, keeping watch up the road for their target. When Heydrich's driver, SS-Oberscharführer Klein, slowed for the tight curve, Jozef Gabčík jumped in front of the car and attempted to fire his machine gun. It jammed.

Heydrich ordered Klein to stop the car, and Heydrich stood to shoot Jozef. Jan threw the grenade toward the back of the convertible. It exploded short of its mark, above the running board in front of the right rear fender. Shrapnel and upholstery fibers drove upward into Heydrich. Gabčík and Kubiš fired their pistols at Heydrich while Klein fired back. All parties missed their shots.

There is some debate as to what happened next. Some sources say Gabčík and Kubiš jumped on their bicycles and made their escape across St. Nicholas bridge. Other reports are that Heydrich ordered Klein to chase the men down on foot, and that Klein pursued Gabčík into a butcher shop, where Gabčík shot Klein twice, wounding the German, before the pair jumped onto a tram. Regardless of how Gabčík and Kubiš got away, they escaped to a safe house, convinced the assassination attempt was a failure.

What the men could not know in those moments right after the attack was that Heydrich had been fatally wounded. The blast from the grenade imbedded the stuffing from Heydrich's car seat deep into his spleen. Bystanders waved down a van that took Heydrich to Bulovka Hospital, where he had surgery to remove his spleen. One week later, Heydrich died.

The official cause of Heydrich's death was recorded as septicemia as a result of bacteria on the upholstery fibers. However, there are at least three other theories. First, the autopsy was more consistent with a pulmonary embolism than with septicemia. The second theory is that the modified anti-tank grenade contained botulism, implanted as part of a UK bioweapons program, and that Heydrich died of botulinum poisoning. It's worth noting he exhibited none of the symptoms of botulism before he died. The third theory is that Heinrich Himmler, Heydrich's direct superior, had his own people whack Heydrich in the hospital. Himmler was reputed to have been both jealous and afraid of Heydrich. When Heydrich was wounded, Himmler sent his personal physicians and insisted that they be the only ones to operate on Heydrich, leading to much speculation on the part of historians.

Himmler, himself, led the search for the assassins. For twenty days, mass arrests and mass executions were the rule, punctuated with massacres. While the numbers are impossible to verify as exact, most sources indicate the Nazis arrested more than thirteen thousand people and executed approximately five thousand more during the reprisals.

During this time on June 9, Himmler plowed the town of Lidice into the ground. Some say the choice of Lidice was arbitrary, and others say Himmler chose Lidice because it was known that the town had been home to several of the Czech officers living in exile in the United Kingdom. The Nazis executed nearly two hundred men and boys above the age of fifteen. They sent the women of Lidice to Ravensbrück concentration camp and took almost one hundred children prisoner. Of the children, eighty-one were deemed racially inappropriate and were exterminated in gas vans in Chelmno. A handful of the children were adopted by German families. Still, Himmler found no trace of the assassins.

Himmler then focused the Nazi might on the hamlet of Ležáky, where some say a radio transmitter left by Silver A team was found. Himmler executed all of the men and women of that town.

After nearly a month of executions and arrests, Himmler then offered a bounty of one million Reichsmarks for information and said that in forty-eight hours, on June 18, he would decimate Prague. At that point, Gabčík and Kubiš's fellow Czech paratrooper, Karel Čurda of the "Out Distance" sabotage group, went to the Gestapo and gave the Nazis the names of the team's local contacts. Čurda also betrayed several safe houses, including that of the Moravec family.

The Gestapo raided the Moravec family home. Mrs. Marie Moravec managed to get to the bathroom and commit suicide with a cyanide capsule. Mr. Alois Moravec, who knew nothing of his family's involvement in the resistance, was taken prisoner with his seventeen-year-old son, Ata. Sources consistently report that the Nazis tortured Ata throughout the day to no avail. At the end of the day, they stupefied the young man with brandy and showed him the head of his mother floating in a fish tank. They told Ata that if he didn't give them the information they wanted, his father would be next. Ata finally gave in and told the Gestapo that his mother had advised him to retreat to the catacombs of the Karel Boromejsky Church if there should ever be trouble.

During the weeks of the manhunt, Gabčík and Kubiš first stayed in safe houses and then hid in the catacombs of the Karel

Boromejsky Church. At least two other Czech patriots were hiding there, Josef Valčík and Lt. Adolf Opálka. Some sources say the other three men of the original seven-man team, Josef Bublík, Jan Hrubý, and Jaroslav Švarc, were there as well. What is not in question is that when the Gestapo surrounded the church on Čurda's information, Gabčík, Kubiš, and the others fought with machine guns and pistols as long as their ammunition held out. Kubiš and Opálka were killed in the loft of the church. Then, the Germans flooded the cellar where the rest were holed up. Gabčík and the others committed suicide to avoid capture.

The church's Bishop Gorazd, concerned about Nazi reprisals among his flock, took full responsibility for the actions in the church, even writing letters to the Nazi authorities. The Nazis arrested him, tortured him, and executed him. The Eastern Orthodox Church then glorified Bishop Gorazd as a martyr.

The Nazis continued their retribution killings in retaliation for Heydrich's assassination. Among those butchered in the slaughter were twenty-four of Jan Kubiš's family, including his father, his siblings, his half-siblings, their spouses, his cousins, his aunts, and his uncles—all murdered by the Germans. Some would say Heydrich's assassination wasn't worth it. However, many would respond that Heydrich was the mastermind behind the slaughter of millions, and, at thirty-eight, he was just getting warmed up.

The Czech Republic and Slovakia have not forgotten Heydrich's oppression or the sacrifices of Jozef Gabčík, Jan Kubiš, and the other men of Operation Anthropoid. Several monuments in the Czech Republic and Slovakia commemorate the mission and its heroes. Streets are named after Kubiš in Prague as well as in several other cities in the Czech Republic, and an entire city in Slovakia, Gabčíkova, is named after Jozef Gabčík. With donations from firefighters, historical societies, and military organizations, as well as from schools and citizens of the Czech Republic, Slovakia, and France, the village of Dolní Vilémovice acquired Jan Kubiš's original home and restored it, making it a museum. Its doors opened on Jan's birthday, June 24, in 2013. The mission where everything went wrong was still an iconic success, as Reinhard Heydrich was the highest-ranking officer in Hitler's cadre to be assassinated during WWII.

In Hrothgar's mead hall, Beowulf said, "Fate will often spare a man if his courage holds." In the case of the assassination of Reinhard Heydrich, the Butcher of Prague, it could be said that Fate spared the mission against all odds because of the courage and determination of Jozef Gabčík, Jan Kubiš, and the team of Operation Anthropoid.

5

ERIC ROBERTS

THE "UNTALENTED" BANK CLERK

SOMETIMES, BEING AN OUTSIDER PROVIDES BOTH COVER AND THE best perspective. This was certainly true in the case of diligent MI-5 operative Eric Roberts. Passed off by the British upper class as an "untalented" bank clerk, Roberts hid behind his seeming mediocrity and succeeded in sabotaging Germany's efforts at recruiting spies in the United Kingdom during WWII. Also, from the perspective of an outsider, he saw his upper-crust espionage coworkers more clearly than they saw themselves and accurately profiled what would come to be known as the Cambridge Five.

Before and during WWII, Germany had a skilled professional intelligence service, the *Abwehr*, which was operated by competent German military personnel. Nazi Party membership was not required to work in the Abwehr, and many did not belong. The predominance of well-educated personnel in the service likely contributed to the organization's lack of enthusiasm for Hitler and the Nazi Party.

The Nazi Party was aware of the Abwehr's lack of Nazi devotion, so Hitler relied heavily on his secret police organization known as the Gestapo, which was led by Heinrich Himmler. Hitler also counted on the *Sicherheitsdienst* ("SD"), which was the intelligence branch of the Nazi Party's *Waffen-Schutzstaffel* ("SS"), also under Himmler's control.

Himmler used his secret police authority against his political opponents within the Nazi Party with great success, and he tried to convince Hitler to let him take command of all German intelligence resources. However, it seems that Hitler was well aware of his senior minions' machinations against each other, and he skillfully encouraged their internal animosity as a way to keep himself safe from any subordinate that might become too powerful.

We now know that the Nazis' distrust of the Abwehr was well founded. As more secret information trickled out to the public after the war, it became apparent to historians that Admiral Canaris and many of his top deputies in the Abwehr not only lacked enthusiasm for the Nazi Party, but they actively plotted against it, including involvement in multiple assassination attempts against Hitler. Based on their lack of trust in the Abwehr, the Gestapo and the SD branch of the SS invested heavily in intelligence operations against the United Kingdom and the Allies.

While understanding the structure and organization of German intelligence operations must have been an ongoing nightmare for an established and traditional organization like MI-5, MI-5 never allowed that to slow them down in their secret war against Axis intelligence operations. Any study of MI-5's wartime operations leads to various interpretations, depending on the student. However, one conclusion that would be difficult for any serious student of espionage to miss would be the fact that, while MI-5 was remarkably ineffective in combating Soviet espionage, they were quite efficient in dealing with the massive intelligence efforts conducted by the Nazis against the United Kingdom.

MI-5 could never be certain which German organization was running which intelligence operation against the United Kingdom, but they *were* certain that *all* German intelligence operations needed to be defeated. On Friday, October 24, 2014, MI-5/MI-6 revealed what had been a tightly-guarded secret about one man's identity, and we learned precisely *how* the Gestapo and SS SD operations were so successfully defeated. In large measure, their defeat was due to an unremarkable bank clerk named Eric Roberts, or at least he appeared to be a bank clerk.

Eric Roberts was born to a humble home in Wivelsfield, England on June 7, 1907. His father was Percival Roberts, who worked for Western Union telegraph. Little is known of Eric's early life other than that he attended free grammar schools. What we do know is that the MI-5 elitists of the time considered him of low birth, and he suffered socially for it in the organization. He was never really accepted in their ranks, even though he was excellent at his job. We suspect this prejudice is at the heart of the scanty information available on Eric Roberts to this day. The upper-class snobs that populated MI-5 were not going to let this low-born chav be known as a hero.

We know, though, that Eric Roberts was a bank clerk by the time he was seventeen, and that MI-5 spymaster Maxwell Knight personally recruited Roberts at some point before WWII. While it's difficult to find information about this exchange, we suspect Knight met Roberts at the bank.

Roberts was so successful in maintaining his cover as a bank clerk while secretly working for MI-5 that when the British War Office requested that his bank employers release him from his work for service in WWII, the bank management resisted. They claimed that Roberts clearly lacked any special talent that would make him particularly useful for the war effort. Apparently, the upper class bankers were at least as classist as the spies of MI-5, and they didn't think much of their low class employee, either. The bank released him to the war effort, never knowing Roberts had been a master spy for quite some time.

Someone in MI-5 leadership understood that countering the German Abwehr would not be enough. That person had the foresight to realize that not only would the Nazi SS SD conduct operations against the United Kingdom, but also that Himmler might use his Gestapo personnel to conduct his own operations against the Allies. In an example of excellent judgment, MI-5 selected Eric Roberts to run an operation against the Nazis. Roberts stopped being a peripheral agent for MI-5 and began working undercover. Still in England, he posed as Jack King, an anti-establishment, pro-Nazi fascist. His mission? To sabotage the Gestapo's efforts at recruiting spies in the United Kingdom.

So how does one bank clerk with nothing more than a suspicion that Germany would recruit more spies in the United Kingdom manage to foil the Gestapo? It occurred to our seemingly dull Roberts that the best way to locate any disloyal, Gestapo-inclined British citizen was to recruit them first.

Roberts set up a system that any pyramid scheme con man would envy. He posed as an undercover Gestapo agent and recruited the would-be traitors. They thought they were working for the Gestapo. Rather than arrest them, MI-5 trained them and used them to recruit their own networks of "Nazi" spies. It dried up the pools of Nazi sympathizers and kept them occupied, hindering the Nazi efforts to find real British traitors to work for them.

Meanwhile, MI-5 and MI-6 both fed a healthy diet of double agents to the Abwehr, the SS SD, and the Gestapo. These double agents presented the Germans with various case files of imaginary agents, producing a plethora of delicious, but usually fake, information. They fed the Germans enough real information to keep them happy, but that real information was just late enough for it to not quite be useful.

Eric Roberts's operations against the Gestapo, along with similar operations by MI-5 and MI-6 against the Abwehr and SS SD, explain why Hitler was so certain that the Allied D-Day invasion would land at Calais rather than at Normandy. Hitler held stubbornly to that conviction against the advice of his General Staff and the advice of his Army Headquarters Staff.

After WWII, Eric Roberts was loaned from MI-5 to MI-6 to work in Vienna as a double agent against the Russians. It was a perilous time in Vienna as the Soviets fought to establish their territory. Austria did not have a solid democratic foundation from which to combat the Komitet Gosudarstvennoy Bezopasnosti ("KGB"), and Roberts's assignment was filled with violence and danger while he worked against the Soviets and their growing hold in Eastern Europe.

Roberts was certain there were Soviet moles in the upper echelons of MI-5/MI-6. When he returned to London from Vienna, he shared his suspicions with MI-5 Deputy Director Guy Liddell and predicted the moles were upper-class graduates of Cambridge or Oxford. Roberts surmised they would do it on a lark, pretending it was socialist ideology, but in reality they would do it out of an inflated sense of self-importance.

MI-5 couldn't digest that, and they unofficially ostracized Roberts for holding that opinion. Of course, the elitists assumed it was a lower class person, and though they later denied it, some of them suspected Roberts himself. All of the upper-class Cambridge spies in the organization did everything they could to push the theory that it was a lower-class infiltrator. In time, Roberts was proven right, and it bothered him that he had unfairly fallen under suspicion. He knew it was because of his "low birth."

Roberts was always private and discreet—traits that undoubtedly helped him in his under-appreciated career at MI-5/MI-6—and little is known about his personal life. We do know that his wife was named Audrey, and that his oldest son was named Maxwell after Maxwell Knight. The three of them, along with Roberts's son Peter and daughter Christa, moved to the Isle of Wight, and then later to Salt Spring Island in Canada. Once there, Roberts pursued a quiet, rural life in the Canadian Pacific. He took up writing and, not surprisingly, he was popular with the local inhabitants. Clearly, the man had a great talent for establishing friendships.

Eric Arthur Roberts passed away in 1972 with no recognition for his fantastic work against the Nazis. Like so many intelligence service personnel, he took his secrets to the grave with him, apparently content with his perceived insignificance in spite of his heroic role in defeating the Nazi plague.

6

IAN FLEMING

THE MAN WHO WROTE THE MYTH

IT IS ARGUABLE THAT NO HOLLYWOOD CHARACTER HAS BEEN MORE enduring or more popular over the decades than Bond—James Bond—novelist Ian Fleming's never shaken, never stirred superstar agent of the UK's MI-6. Watching the Bond movies would likely leave viewers thinking that Fleming possessed a good imagination and little or no knowledge of the grueling, tedious, and dangerous work done by real life intelligence operatives. Bond's lavish spending on equipment and accommodations and the hours he wiles away tossing money around in posh casinos surrounded by lonely, glamorous women would make average MI-6 employees chuckle to themselves. But while Fleming chose to write far-fetched plots that didn't always bother to tie together details in a realistic way, he never let on that he was, himself, a spymaster who led two of the most successful teams of WWII.

Ian Lancaster Fleming, the second of four sons, was born to a wealthy Scottish-English family on May 28, 1908. Some sources say the family traces back to an Elizabethan intelligence operative, John Bond, whose motto was *Non Sufficit Orbis*, or, "The world is not enough."

In 1910, Fleming's father became a Member of Parliament. He then served as an officer in the Queen's Own Oxfordshire Hussars during WWI and was killed in combat on the Western Front in 1917. Ian was nine years old. Winston Churchill wrote the obituary for Ian's father, and it was published in *The Times*. "He was most earnest and sincere in his desire to make things better for the great body of the people." Ian kept a copy of this obituary on his bedroom wall throughout his life.

Young Ian was sent to Eton. Sources contain contradicting information about this time in his life. Some say he was the greatest Etonian of all time, and others say he was a mediocre student who excelled at athletics. We ascribe to the latter school of thought. Either way, he served as co-editor of the college magazine, *The Wyvern*, which published his first short story, *The Ordeal of Caryl St. George*.

Fleming left his studies at Eton a term early to prepare to enter Sandhurst Military Academy. However, he didn't complete the course at Sandhurst. Pro-Fleming sources aren't going to be happy with us for saying this, but after less than a year at Sandhurst, Fleming contracted gonorrhea. This seems to be evidence that Ian may not have been in his room studying all the time. Staff were apparently pretty sure he was not in the library, rowing on the river, or on the obstacle course when he contracted it, either. In fact, contracting a venereal disease was a somewhat unique achievement for a Sandhurst cadet. Fleming moved on.

It entered Fleming's mind, or at least his mother's mind, that he should work in the British Foreign Office, so he traveled to Kitzbühel in Austria to perfect his abilities in German and French. He enjoyed his time there and later described it in a letter to a friend as "that golden time when the sun always shone." After a year, he went on to study German and French at the

Munich University in Germany and the Geneva University in Switzerland.

The brilliant Fleming mysteriously failed the Foreign Office exam in 1931 and did not opt to retest. Instead, he took a position as a journalist with the Reuters news service and spent part of 1933 in Moscow. In retrospect, Fleming's failure on the Foreign Office exam may have been arranged by MI-6 recruiters. It kept him "clean" of association with the British Foreign Office, perhaps enabling deep cover peacetime work for the British intelligence community.

Though Fleming reportedly enjoyed his two years as a journalist with Reuters, he found, like almost all writers, that writing rarely provides the lifestyle into which he had been born. Fleming moved on to become a banker and a stockbroker. It was during this time in 1934 that he met Lady Ann O'Neill, wife of Irish peer Shane O'Neill, who would become his paramour in 1939, and eventually his wife.

Also in 1939, shortly before the beginning of WWII, Fleming accepted a reserve commission as a subaltern in Britain's renowned Black Watch regiment and became assistant to Rear Admiral John Godfrey, the Director of Naval Intelligence of the Royal Navy. During this period with Adm. Godfrey, Fleming helped formulate a plan of countermeasures to defend Gibraltar in case Spain should decide to align with the Nazis and attack it. This plan was known as Operation Goldeneye.

In contrast to the snail's pace promotion world of the British Navy, Fleming quickly rose to the rank of commander. His imagination served him well in naval intelligence, and in 1942, he commanded an elite special intelligence force known as 30 Assault Unit, or "30AU," which was specially trained in intelligence gathering techniques. Fleming selected men for this unit that he felt had the intelligence and sophistication to recognize valuable information that normal commandos might not notice, and they operated in Europe with great success.

Fleming also helped found the highly successful "T Force" for the purpose of recovering Nazi technology from the collapsing Nazi empire at the end of the war. Their task was to get to German technology before the Soviets or the Americans could get to it. The Nazis had developed several new weapons in the fields of rocket science, chemistry, jet engine and submarine engineering, and electronics that the Germans no longer had the industrial infrastructure to produce, or that they could not produce in significant numbers. T Force used a variety of sources to locate and acquire these technologies. More than once, Fleming's mission inadvertently found him behind enemy lines, and he had to work his way out and back to safety. In the end, T Force was more successful than anyone imagined was possible. Anyone but Fleming, that is.

Fleming was also part of Operation Mincemeat, which helped convince Hitler that the Allied Invasion would take place in Greece and Sardinia in 1943 rather than in Sicily. The British planted false information on the corpse of a British serviceman and arranged for it to wash up onto the coast of Spain. The Germans picked up the body with the official documents and were fooled.

Fleming never spoke of his war-time activities to outsiders. Some say Allied commanders misused the 30AU before and during the main Normandy invasion, resulting in heavy casualties, and that this deeply impacted Fleming. To strangers and journalists, Fleming always minimized his war experiences with vague stories of a paper-pushing office life.

Near the end of WWII, Fleming attended an Anglo-American intelligence conference in Kingston, Jamaica. It was then that he decided that after the war was over, he would move to Jamaica and write "the spy story to end all spy stories." In 1947, he followed through and bought an old donkey racetrack on Oracabessa Bay. He named it "Goldeneye." There are several theories about the origins of that name, but we favor the idea that Fleming took it from his first field task, Operation Goldeneye.

After WWII, Fleming took a job as the foreign manager of London newspaper *Sunday Times*. Ann O'Neill had been widowed before the end of the war, but for their own reasons, she and Fleming did not marry at that time. Instead, she married Lord Rothermere and continued her love affair with Fleming. Then, in 1951, she became pregnant with Fleming's child. Lord Rothermere divorced her. When Fleming sat down and wrote his first James Bond novel, *Casino Royale*, in January 1952, he joked that it was to distract himself from his impending nuptials. He married Ann in March, 1952, and their only child, Caspar, was born on August 11.

Fleming spent the first three months of each of the next twelve years until 1964 writing Bond novels at Goldeneye. *Casino Royale* was published in 1953 by Jonathan Cape in the United Kingdom, to be followed by *Live and Let Die, Moonraker, Diamonds Are Forever, From Russia with Love, Dr. No, Goldfinger, For Your Eyes Only, Thunderball, The Spy Who Loved Me, On Her Majesty's Secret Service, You Only Live Twice, The Man with the Golden Gun,* and *Octopussy and the Living Daylights*. Though Fleming is most famous for his Bond series, he also wrote *The Diamond Smugglers, Thrilling Cities,* and *Chitty Chitty Bang Bang*.

The first attempt to bring Bond to the screen was in 1954, when CBS produced an adaptation of *Casino Royale* for television under the name *Climax!* The show starred Barry Nelson as "Jimmy Bond." It didn't work out.

Then, in 1961, Albert R. Broccoli and Harry Saltzman teamed up to bring *Dr. No* to the big screen, which was the beginning of the longest-running, most successful movie franchise in history. The dozens of Bond films over the decades are not only bold and exciting, they are a reflection of the last sixty years of changing social issues and attitudes toward war, space travel, feminism, realism in film, and exactly what constitutes a hero. The Bond character continues to evolve in step with changing social values and the politics of Big Media.

One charming story of Fleming is that he heard about a party to celebrate the production of a Bond movie that was made without his input. The party was held in the pool area of a hilltop mansion overlooking the Atlantic in the Bahamas, and it was crawling with British royals and other VIPs. The security effort was intense and included troops of guards with machine guns and guard dogs. Fleming allegedly slipped in through the security cordons, strolled through the crowd, and accepted a glass of champagne from a waiter. A few of the movie people who knew him recognized him, and, as a murmur grew in the crowd, Fleming stepped out of the light and vanished.

On August 12, 1964—his son's twelfth birthday—Ian Lancaster Fleming died of a heart attack in Kent, England, at the age of fifty-six. He is interred next to his wife, Ann Fleming (1913-81), and Caspar Robert Fleming (1952-75), in the village of Sevenhampton, England, near the Welsh border.

We wonder if, when Fleming set out to write "the spy story that would end all spy stories," he ever knew that he had done exactly that. He set the standard by which all that follow are measured. We have no doubt, though, that his real life exploits in espionage far exceeded those of his mythical creation.

7

BILLY WAUGH
PERSISTENCE PERSONIFIED

Espionage field work is tough, whether it's skydiving into the ocean to swim through murky, shark-infested waters and blow up enemy targets, or watching the same door for months on end from the window of a condemned Third World hellhole. Try to find the definition of that kind of tough in any accurate dictionary, and you'll find a picture of Billy Waugh, a man who served in several wars and was on teams that found Carlos the Jackal and Osama Bin Laden.

Billy Waugh was born on December 1, 1929, in Bastrop, Texas. Always industrious, he got a job manning pumps at a gas station at the age of eight and went on to become the popcorn jockey at a movie theater before the age of twelve.

In 1945, at the age of sixteen, Billy met some wounded Marines who were home from the war in the Pacific. It was then he decided he was going to join the Marine Corps. He'd heard that he could sign up in California, and he started hitchhiking there to do so. A police officer spotted him in Las Cruces, New Mexico, pulled him in, and locked him up at the jail. Billy persuaded the officer to let him talk to the Marine recruiter from Deming, who did not believe Billy's lie that he was eighteen. Billy was forced to choose between the prospect of living in the Las Cruces jail or facing his mother. A tough choice, but he called his mother. She wired him bus fare to get home so she could tan his hide.

After that, Billy decided to stay in high school. He graduated with a 4.0 and joined the US Army paratroopers in 1948. He completed Airborne school the same year.

In 1951, Billy fought in the Korean War with the 187th Airborne Regimental Combat Team. Information on this period of his life is rather scant. There's a lot Billy doesn't say about it, and we aren't the type to pry—at least not with one of our own.

After the Korean War, Billy was accepted for Army Special Forces training. In 1954, he earned his green beret and joined the 10th Special Forces in Germany. Little has been published about Waugh's time with the 10th in Germany, but he likely spent much of it preparing for work behind Warsaw Pact lines and for the possibility that the Soviet Army might cross the Fulda Gap into West Germany.

In 1961, US President Kennedy was optimistic about what US Army Special Forces teams might achieve in Vietnam. Billy Waugh was one of the many remarkable American soldiers who proved JFK right. That same year, Waugh left the United States for a quick tour of duty in Southeast Asia and forgot to tell anyone that he would be gone for nearly a decade. He served on small Special Forces detachments known then as A-teams, working on counter-insurgency operations against the Viet Cong, North Vietnamese ("NVA"), and other communist forces in South Vietnam and Laos.

In 1965, Billy lead an advance patrol of a Civilian Irregular Defense Group to what had previously been identified as an NVA camp, where it was believed there were fewer than two hundred NVA soldiers. Unfortunately, the camp had since been reinforced by both NVA and Chinese forces and contained over four thousand enemy troops.

After inflicting heavy casualties on the enemy, Waugh was badly wounded in his head and legs and left for dead by the counterattacking communist forces. Waugh later regained consciousness and made it back to where his team maintained a defensive position. He was successfully evacuated to a field hospital. In spite of his severe wounds, Waugh survived and underwent reconstructive surgeries and physical therapy at Walter Reed Hospital. Everyone understood that Billy's US Army career was over. Everyone except Billy, that is.

Remarkably, he regained enough of his health and ability to avoid a medical discharge from the Army. Everyone then knew that with his long combat experience and years of training, he would make a fine administrative Non-Commissioned Officer. However, Billy had something else in mind. He wrangled a transfer back to Vietnam to serve in a Special Forces Headquarters. After getting himself to Vietnam, it wasn't long before he got away from a desk and back into the jungle with combat teams.

Billy joined the elite, inter-service Studies and Observation Group in 1966. This group frequently engaged in successful, hair-raising schemes to harm the NVA and Viet Cong Guerillas while assisting Laotians, Cambodians, and rural Vietnamese in developing defensive skills.

In 1970, Billy conducted an armed *training* mission in enemy territory using a High Altitude Low Opening ("HALO") jump. In 1971, he took part in the first recorded *operational* mission into enemy territory—a special reconnaissance mission—using a HALO jump. And that is all we will say about that.

After the Vietnam War, Billy retired from the US Army. During his Army career, he was decorated with numerous medals, including the Silver Star, the Legion of Merit, four Bronze Stars, four Purple Hearts, four Army Commendation Medals (with V for valor), and an incredible fourteen Army Air Medals. If not for the clandestine nature of so many of his combat missions in Southeast Asia, he likely would have received multiple awards of the Distinguished Service Cross, or possibly a Medal of Honor. We doubt that would have mattered much to Billy. He got what he had wanted all along—a chance to serve his country and to defend freedom.

After spending so many years in combat and suffering so many severe injuries, a reasonable man would have spent his retirement years gardening and perhaps teaching Sunday School. Fortunately for the United States, Billy Waugh cannot be accused of being anything like "reasonable."

Waugh's idea of retirement was to spend decades in the CIA, both on the employee side of the shop and the contractor side of the shop. Between his various periods of service with the CIA, he used his "fun time" to earn a Master of Science in Criminal Justice from Texas State University.

Note to graduate students: Stop whining! What you're doing is what people like Billy Waugh do for vacation.

Waugh's decades of service for the CIA included time in corners of Africa and Central Asia where reasonable men don't go. As a result, Billy was instrumental in locating and tracking Ilich Ramirez Sanchez, a.k.a. Carlos the Jackal, in his refuge in Khartoum, Sudan. Thanks to him and his coworkers, the United States was able to give France the details concerning Carlos's location and activities, which allowed the French to capture and imprison Carlos in France without any diplomatic entanglements for the

United States. We have more about this manhunt in *Spycraft: Essentials*, and while we certainly recommend our own book, we highly recommend that you read Billy's autobiography, *Hunting the Jackal*, for the full account, along with so many other fascinating stories.

While Billy was in Khartoum looking for Carlos the Jackal, he just happened to stumble across another infamous terrorist—Osama Bin Laden. As Billy tells it, he was out jogging in Khartoum and spotted the rat-bastard Bin Laden in his compound. Billy made it part of his routine to jog by Bin Laden's compound every day. Waugh and his team tracked the dirtbag and were prepared to kill him. Unfortunately, they did not receive permission from President Clinton to do so.

After Bin Laden's followers committed the 9/11 atrocities against the United States, a youthful 71-year-old Billy was among that small handful of Americans who jumped into Afghanistan to coordinate with the Northern Alliance against the radical Islamic Taliban. They succeeded quickly with a remarkably low cost in lives and wealth. The fact that the United States later squandered its success by propping up a weak, corrupt facade of a government in Kabul while failing to gain real cooperation from the splintered government in Pakistan in no way lessons the outstanding achievements of the CIA personnel who led the charge against the Taliban.

The full extent of Billy Waugh's past and current activities remains unknown, but we do know this: Billy Waugh asks for nothing and continues to give his all. We extend our gratitude to Billy Waugh and to his many fellow Vietnam Era veterans who have done so much for the Intelligence Community and for this nation.

You can learn more about Billy Waugh at his website, SGM Billy Waugh, http://billywaugh.net. There, you can find his excellent

books, *Hunting the Jackal* and *Isaac Camacho, an American Hero.*
Prepare to be amazed.

8

FERNANDO "X"

EL TIGRE CON COJONES IMMENSOS

IF YOU ARE A CASTRO-APOLOGIST, THIS CHAPTER WILL SURELY confuse and stress you. For the rest of our readers, if you ever visit Key West, Florida, stroll to the south end of the island. You will find there a monument heralding the southernmost point in the contiguous forty-eight states. That monument will tell you that Cuba is ninety miles to the south. The monument is mistaken. Cuba is ninety-five miles south. It could be corrected, but we hope it remains inaccurate. In its current condition it serves, albeit accidentally, as a monument to the many popular misconceptions that Western journalists and politicians harbor about the reality of Cuba.

Rather than focus on the many grim aspects of life in Cuba, we prefer to remember the brave Cubans who have risked their lives in the hope of bringing freedom and justice to their island nation. At this point, most of them would settle for just the freedom. One of those brave Cubans was a man Holmes was honored to know and call friend. In this chapter, we will call him Fernando "X."

Fernando was older than Holmes. The last time Holmes saw him, he told Holmes that he would not live to see Cuba free. Fernando said in Spanish, "The son of a bitch assassin Fidel will outlive me. Well, that's life. I have done the best I could, brother." Holmes knew he was right.

Fernando was in poor health and didn't look like he had much left in him. Holmes knew the look and was not ready to admit it, so he lied. With a few of his favorite Spanish curses, Holmes told Fernando that Satan couldn't keep Fidel out of Hell forever, and that the bastard would surely die soon. They laughed.

Fernando looked at Holmes, and said, "It's okay, *hermanito*. I can't stay forever. Take good care of your children. Give them the love that I won't be here to give them. I would have liked to. It was my one way of thanking you." Holmes wanted to cry, but he knew he owed Fernando something better than that, so he just smiled and assured his friend that he would, and that Holmes's family would not forget him. They haven't, and they won't. Neither will the people of Cuba.

Six decades ago, on an October afternoon in 1958, Fernando's life was about to get more exciting. The teenage revolutionary wanted a rifle and grenades and some excitement on one of the many raids that were being conducted against the incompetent dictator Fulgencio Bautista's clown-ocracy. Instead, Fernando was equipped with soap and sponges in his personal battle against the dirty pots and pans in his camp's kitchen. He was not enjoying the revolution much. He wondered if he shouldn't have listened to his mother and stayed home to tend the pigs and chickens. He was starting to miss his boring, pleasant home life.

For reasons unknown, the group's *comandante* decided to bring "El Niño," the boy, along on the day's raid. Fernando remembered being excited. He intended to make a name for himself. He had insisted to his cohorts that his nickname was "El Tigre," the tiger. His cohorts were even more insistent that his nickname would remain El Niño. Before the day ended, they were calling

Fernando "El Tigre Con Cojones Immensos," the tiger withimmense balls.

Fernando was given a captured American-made M-1 Garand. He was small and the rifle was heavy. Too heavy. The group decided he should carry a much lighter captured American-made M-1 carbine. The fact that they had no ammo for it was a disappointment for Fernando. His cohorts assured him that they were just going to occupy a recently-abandoned police station, and that there would be plenty of ammo there for everyone. Fernando was supposed to stay behind everyone else until they secured the building. The five revolutionaries climbed into a Chevrolet sedan and drove to the supposedly abandoned police station, but the best-laid plans of mice and revolutionaries . . .

They arrived at the plaza where the police station was located and jumped out of the Chevrolet with much bravado. Oddly, none of the locals came out to cheer or jeer. The revolutionaries walked toward the front door of the station, and a shot rang out. The round kicked up dirt near them. They all jumped for cover—all of them except El Tigre. The fifteen-year-old Fernando stood his ground with his empty rifle.

The somewhat loyalist police retreated to the roof top. They had ammo in their weapons. Fernando wasn't sure how many police there were, nor what they had to fight with, but he stood his ground without flinching. He stared up at the policeman that stared down from the parapet of the roof. The policeman said they didn't want to kill anyone, and that the revolutionaries should all just get in their car, leave, and not return. Four of the five revolutionaries thought it sounded like a great deal and jumped in the car. They yelled to El Tigre to get the hell back in the car. El Tigre didn't budge.

The policeman vanished from the parapet for a moment. A few seconds later, one of the police returned to the edge of the roof and yelled down, "Let us leave and you can have the station. Just let us leave without any shooting." The cops were either impressed by the kid's courage, or they just didn't want to shoot a child on behalf of a government that they never much liked. The revolutionary *comandante* got out of the car and yelled up his agreement. No shots were fired that day, but a hero of the revolution was born. Fernando was something of a celebrity—a teenage superhero.

A few months later, Cuban dictator Bautista realized that neither his fellow Latin-American despots nor the United States was going to back him up. He hit the road. Fernando and his friends celebrated. They were free. They could build a free and just society.

In the following months, as Fidel Castro consolidated his grip on power, inconvenient dissenters died publicly or vanished. Then, as Fernando grew into adulthood, like many of his revolutionary cohorts, he grew disillusioned with the new regime. All he could see in Cuba was less freedom, more misery, and a vanishing hope for his people and country. The new Bastard in Chief Castro somehow managed to be even worse at governing than the previous Bastard in Chief Bautista had been.

With all the standard Soviet-style rhetoric and Soviet specialists assisting, Fidel and his elite friends assured the public that once they overcame the mostly-imaginary aggression of the evil American imperialists, they would all build their great socialist paradise. The new president of the American imperialists, John F. Kennedy, radically trimmed back the planned support of exiled Cubans for an impending invasion of Cuba. Worse still, the operation had been penetrated by the Cuban government. Eventually, against the advice of the US military, a half-hearted invasion occurred at the wrong location, the Bay of Pigs.

The previous president, Dwight D. Eisenhower, was an "invade Normandy with everything we can send" sort of man. He had been successful using that strategy when invading Normandy. However, the new president was a "do way more with way less" PT boat veteran. He had been somewhat successful with that strategy in the wildly dangerous waters of the Solomon Islands. In Cuba, the "way less" was way too little. The invasion failed. Fidel celebrated his "grand victory" over the feeble attempt.

Eventually, Fernando, whose first priority was always the Cuban people, decided it was time to resist against the new despots. He did. He helped the United States try to help Cuba. As a revolutionary celebrity, Fernando had status and access to many top members of Fidel's regime. This gave Fernando a great deal of valuable information about the regime's intentions.

Through a like-minded ex-revolutionary cohort, Fernando was able to make contact with the US Intelligence Community, and for several years, he risked his life by sharing valuable information with the United States. We will not elaborate on the nature or extent of that information. Suffice to say that, thanks to Fernando's efforts, numerous Cuban dissidents were able to escape from Cuba and move to the United States or Spain. Many of these people would have been tortured and even executed if not for Fernando's quiet help. He saved many lives and asked for nothing in return.

It couldn't last forever. Fernando was betrayed. He ran for his life and hid, but he was eventually captured. To Fidel and his monsters, Fernando was a traitor. To the United States, he was a hero. Fernando expected to be shot. Instead, he was sent to the infamous political prison on Isla de Juventud to rot in grim conditions for a few decades.

Day after day, year after year, Fernando wondered if he would live to feel the sun on his skin before he died. One day, the prison authorities caught him writing in a hidden journal. They broke several bones in each of his hands. He received no medical attention. For the rest of Fernando's life, his hands caused him great pain. He survived the torture and abuse, though many did not.

Nearly twenty years ago, by methods that Holmes will not elaborate on or ever admit to, Fernando was able to leave the prison on Isla de Juventud and come to the United States. Along with several others of Holmes's favorite Cuban exiles, they became close friends. In poor health, Fernando lived a sparse life here. Holmes and his friends helped him a bit. He more than deserved it. He was poor in American terms, but in terms of spirit, he was a rich man with much to offer the world. Holmes knew he was blessed to call Fernando a friend.

One Christmas, Holmes was home for the holidays and brought Fernando to his house to join his family and many of their mutual Cuban friends. Fernando had saved a few dollars from his tight budget to buy Holmes's children gifts. They were poorly wrapped by his tortured hands, but Holmes thought they were the most beautiful gifts his kids had ever received. They loved Fernando and understood. They were touched by the gifts. Holmes's wife had knitted Fernando a nice sweater and scarf, Holmes's father gave him a gift certificate for groceries, and Holmes gave him a case of decent rum. Fernando was thrilled, and he used a couple shots before bedtime to deaden the pain in his hands enough to sleep for a while.

One of the party attendees, the brilliant Doctor Jesus Jose Acea Rodriguez, was also in attendance that evening. He, too, had taken risks to try to help Cuba. Jesus asked Fernando to recount his well-known heroic events. Fernando described in brilliant detail the events of the day when he earned the name El Tigre. Holmes could smell the salt air of the Cuban coast and feel the

Cuban earth beneath his feet as he imagined the cop firing that shot.

Then Fernando told them a previously unshared detail of that battle. He had not budged when the police fired because he was scared stiff and couldn't move. The police apparently misjudged the situation. Fortunately, everyone else except for Fernando misunderstood, as well. El Tigre was forever a hero because he was frozen in fear. They laughed a long time as Fernando pantomimed his famous stand-off. They loved him. Everyone did. . . . Everyone except Fidel Castro and his regime.

Before driving Fernando home the next morning, Holmes took his Garand rifle out of his gun safe and slipped it into his car. When they arrived at Fernando's apartment, Holmes told Fernando he had waited a long time for the rifle he wanted. Holmes gave the M-1 to him. Fernando laughed. He was thrilled. They hugged.

Holmes often sits at the same antique table that his family and friends sat at that beautiful Christmas night, and he misses Fernando and the many Cubans that now reside in his past. They stood up for freedom at a great cost. Fernando once told Holmes to never give up hope for Cuba and to teach his children to understand that in the end, evil will always fail because freedom and justice are natural and right. Fernando believed that, and we do, too.

The Caribbean Sea holds the blood of many brave Cubans. Most of the many Cuban people that have secretly risked their lives in the hope of bringing Cuba a better future will never be known. Many did not live to see Cuba free. We might not live that long, either, but for all Holmes's days, he will hold onto his hope and remember his many beautiful Cuban cohorts. We hope that you will, as well.

9

ANALYSTS

THE HEROES WHO DON'T MAKE THE MOVIES

ONE PARTICULAR GROUP OF DEDICATED PROFESSIONALS ARE AT THE very heart of intelligence work. Most of them will likely never receive a medal, a handshake from a US president, or even much of a "thank you" on their way out the door after decades of hard work and loyalty. You may have met some of them, but unless you are in their need-to-know zone, they probably never told you what they did.

You might live next door to one. They will discuss gardening, sports, PTA meetings and lots of other topics with you, and they will be happy to tell you about their "job," just not their real job. The higher they are in their field and the more critical their work is, the less you will know about it. The chances are that long after they retire, they will hold to their cover story. The more exciting their career was, the more mundane their cover will be.

The dedicated intelligence professionals that we are referring to are those that we collectively refer to as "analysts." They sound every bit as humdrum as Wall Street bond analysts, but they aren't. In the military aviation world, bomber pilots are fond of saying, "Fighter pilots make movies; we make history." Intelligence analysts might say, "Covert operatives make movies; we make history." They would be fairly well justified in doing so. All the money and risk that goes into collection is for naught without their contribution.

Those in the covert operations side of the business may at times undervalue the work of analysts, and at times operatives become impatient with them. From their point of view, they found it, saw it, recorded it, photographed it, and at times even blew it up. It might seem like the intelligence picture in front of them is as clear as a sunny day. If not that, then at least as clear as the best technology will illuminate a dark night or see through a smog-filled day in Beijing. So why, then, would the analysts fret or question the operatives' interpretations?

For example, when standing at a window in a foreign country, observing a major terrorist come and go day after day, operatives might wonder why action has not been taken. From where they stand at that moment, they cannot see that the analytical team is also receiving valid information from a wide range of other sources. The field operatives may have solidly identified a dangerous jihadi scumbag. They may have a team in good position to gift said scumbag with his seventy-two virgins—which are probably Chinese blow up dolls. They may even be in a position to make sure that the local cops report it as an attack by a rival group of jihadi scumbags. At the same time, some drone pilot sitting in a cargo container thousands of miles away might also be wondering why he can't go ahead and fire. Let's get this party started!

More experienced field spies know better than to make assumptions about what's going on "back at the office." While those in the field are ready to rumble, an analytical team may have good reason to believe that the scumbag in question is soon going to attend a meeting with a dozen higher-ranking scumbags, and if everyone is patient, then they can arrange a much more profitable use of a $25,000 JDAM bomb or a $110,000 drone-fired Hellfire missile. At any price point, why settle for one dead bad guy if you can kill or capture a dozen? More experienced operatives have learned that there is always more at stake than what is in front of a single team or even entire groups of teams in a region.

It can be difficult to remain patient when suffering from a few exotic diseases in a filthy, dangerous corner of the world where cruise ships don't visit, wondering how the wife and children are doing at home. Those in the field can't contact them. It would be nice to go home. They might start telling jokes amongst themselves about the analysts, deputy directors, and various politicians. They have to keep themselves laughing somehow. But let us assume then that in spite of the jokes, the teams remain patient.

If the risks and the patience pay off, and a dozen jihadi scumbags find themselves trying to inflate plastic blowup dolls in Hell, the operatives will all be happy, and that happiness traces back to the analysts. If the success story is shared with the media, the public will envision Navy SEALs, Green Berets, fighter pilots, cranky ill-mannered spies, or any other brand of heroes as having scored another victory. Few members of the public and even fewer members of the government will stop to consider that without long hours, days, weeks, months, and in many cases years of grueling work on the part of anonymous analysts in the background, the success would not have been possible.

Let us dispel a few popular myths about analysts.

- **They are analysts because they couldn't cut it in "the field."**

No. They are analysts because they have high IQs, a strong work ethic, stable egos, trustworthiness, the ability to remain objective at all times regardless of their passions, and a dogged devotion to the pursuit of the truth.

- **Analysts are all alike and all do similar work.**

No. Analysts are quite varied in education, skill sets, personalities, and jobs. Some might be brilliant scientists, engineers, or computer experts. They might analyze scientific data collected in the field, or they might invent new methods of analysis. Some might specialize in the personalities of foreign leaders, such as Vladimir Putin, and spend years examining every available piece of information about them. Others might specialize in counterterrorism or counterintelligence. There are about a dozen main types of analysts, and various groups within each type. They work together as needed to meet the day's demands for intelligence.

- **Analysts spend their careers doing the same thing on the same team.**

No. The CIA and other organizations are certain that it is best for analysts to change teams after a few years so that they will not lose perspective or start missing valuable clues. A career analyst will have worked in several different areas of focus.

- **Analysts never go to the mythical and glorious "field."**

They sometimes do, and some more than others. At times, a particular analyst might be the best person for a meeting with an agent or potential agent. Analysts also may take assignments at US embassies or other foreign locations.

- **Analysts never face danger.**

We wish that were true. It is not. What do you think Team Jihadi would pay for the location of the person that led the hunt for Bin Laden? What do you think they would do with that information? Before SEAL Team Six could fly to that compound in Pakistan, a large and dedicated team led by a brilliant man worked for years to get a solid location on Osama. Many lunches were skipped. Nights at home were skipped. Vacations were missed. Sleep was lost, and who can even calculate the thousands of hours of unpaid overtime that those team members worked? They wouldn't call it "overtime." They wouldn't call it anything. They won't even tell you they were there doing the work.

Angelina Jolie will never play one on the big screen. There will be no action figures portraying them in their business casual with their PowerPoint slides. Their pictures will never become social media memes of cool invulnerability. Nevertheless, they are the glue that binds the Intelligence Community together—the hub that informs the wheel in its direction. So we finish this section of The Good by remembering the thousands of unsung heroes that dedicate their lives to the difficult process of turning data and evidence into useful intelligence.

THE BAD

———

THE CAMBRIDGE FIVE

Anthony Blunt
"The Fourth Man"

Guy Burgess
The Playboy

Donald Duart Maclean
The Sincere One

Kim Philby
The Man Who Caused a Thousand Deaths

John Cairncross
The One That Got Away

———

Christopher Boyce & Andrew Daulton Lee
The Falcon and The Snowman

Bradley/Breanna/Chelsea Manning
The Soldier that Never Should Have Been One

Robert Hanssen
At the Corner of Ego and Treason

10

THE CAMBRIDGE FIVE

FROM THE END OF WWII IN 1945 UNTIL THE FALL OF THE UNITED Socialist Soviet Republics government in Russia in 1991, Western nations faced off with the Soviet Union, its allies, its captive satellite states, and eventually China in what became known as the "Cold War." The Soviet Union, led by the ruthless Joseph Stalin, perceived that it was its duty to spread communism throughout the world. For their part, Western nations governed by democratic republics were committed to keeping the entire world from falling under communist domination. However, no one wanted a "hot war" so close on the heels of WWII. As a result, the fighting was done through proxy wars, espionage, and covert special operations.

Most of the participants of the Cold War conflict will remain forever unknown, but there are notable exceptions, and they are worth examining. One of the most infamous groups of spies rooted out in the West is now called The Cambridge Five. When they were first exposed in 1951, only two had been identified, Guy Burgess and Donald Duart Maclean, and a long struggle ensued to expose the "third man." Eventually, British MI-6 agent Kim

Philby was discovered, and they became the Unholy Trinity, but British MI-5 and the US CIA remained convinced that a piece was missing. In time, the fourth and fifth men, Anthony Blunt and John Cairncross, were exposed. They had all been recruited from Cambridge University in England, hence the term "The Cambridge Five."

When the West purchased documents from within the Kremlin after the fall of the Soviet Union, it became evident that the Soviet Union had been stunningly successful with its efforts at the elite university, and the term "The Cambridge Forty" would have been closer to accurate than the Cambridge Five. However, since this is a book and not an encyclopedia, we will only discuss the most famous five of that plethora of traitors.

Today, when we look back from half a century, it seems absurd that so many spoiled children of the United Kingdom's privileged upper class would turn on their own to assist Josef Stalin in his dream to create world-wide communism. These were, after all, children of the very families that had the most to lose if Stalin and his pals ever achieved their stated aims. To better understand the Cambridge connivers, it helps to consider the world that they came from and what some of their beliefs might have been.

While we in the West often think of the communist revolution in Russia as a distinctly Russian event, it was, in fact, started as part of a broader international communist movement. Before Lenin and the communist party in Russia were able to consolidate their power and defeat the imperialist Russian forces, communist parties were well established in underground networks in England, France, Italy, and Spain. Other nations in Europe and the Americas, including the United States, had underground communist networks, as well, but they were smaller and less successful.

Not all communist sympathizers were underground. For many people in the early twentieth century, communism was a philosophy that seemed to hold out hope for the less-privileged members of society. Individuals could be "communist" without anyone automatically assuming that they were violent revolutionaries or disloyal to their own nations. By the 1930s, though, most literate people around the world began to take a less sympathetic view toward communism. Enough information had come out of the Soviet police state for "communism" to become a synonym for "oppressive government and ruthless totalitarian control."

Though the concept of communism lost its luster for most Westerners, Western governments were not always successful in providing the majority of voters in democratic nations with completely attractive alternatives. The horrors of WWI, followed by the world economic depression of the 1920s and 1930s, likely contributed to a lack of faith in Western capitalism and democratic governments. This provided an opening for the Soviets to recruit agents willing to betray their own countries.

The Soviets realized early on that while they had blue collar communist recruits aplenty in Europe and, to a lesser extent, in the United States, they needed to recruit some future movers and shakers from among the European and American elite. The disenchanted miners, dock workers, and untalented poets might have been loyal communists and might at times have been useful, but few of them were likely to ever rise to the halls of power in Japan, Europe, Australia, New Zealand, and the Americas. As a result, Cambridge University was one of the primary recruiting targets for the Soviet intelligence organizations.

From the Soviet point of view, the liberal and supposedly hedonistic culture at Cambridge made it a perfect breeding ground for spies. We're not sure just how hedonistic the culture was at Cambridge or at the off-campus social circles of its faculty and students, but the Soviets were highly successful at their recruiting attempts among the Cambridge elites.

There is a vast and tiresome mythology surrounding the lives of the infamous Cambridge gang while they were students, Cairncross excepted. The myths revolve around supposed live witness accounts as to who attended which particular drunken, homosexual/bisexual/other exotic sexual orgies that the youngsters might have organized in their residences or in their fertile imaginations. Much debate has surrounded the topic of who bedded whom first, second, third, etc. That four-dimensional sexual jigsaw puzzle has been examined by many in an attempt to help determine who actually recruited whom at what time. We sincerely pity the poor bastards at MI-5 who spent years trying to complete that jigsaw puzzle.

We will likely never get an accurate image of . . . well, let us rephrase this with a more merciful sentence. We will probably never know the precise chronology of events that led to the creation of the espionage "menage a quarante" of Blunt, Burgess, Philby, and Maclean that resulted from the extracurricular activities of the communistically-enamored clique at Cambridge. Certain themes seem to be consistent from the available information, and when one examines the verifiable facts and the many legends, a picture of Anthony Blunt as an early central figure rises from the toxic historical swamp that they left behind.

In contrast, Blunt claimed that Guy Burgess had recruited him to the communist cause after Burgess graduated from Cambridge. However, Blunt's version of the early days of the Cambridge gang seems to be a fabrication that suited whatever his purposes were from day to day. The fact that Blunt and others changed the details about the pertinent events at Cambridge during their post-exposure decades may indicate that Blunt was mouthing whatever a Soviet controller instructed him to repeat.

While changing one's story can lead to a lack of credibility with some literate segments of the British and Western public, it was a common and trouble-free practice in the Soviet Union. Until the 1970s, some Soviet controllers and their bosses apparently failed to understand the differences in public reactions between the Soviet Union and the Western audiences and governments. At times, the Soviets clearly played too freely by changing details in cover stories.

One of the reasons why this might have occurred is that the Soviets may have been overwhelmed by the complexities of the relationships and the interdependence that they created with their success in recruiting so many interconnected operatives at Cambridge. In the age before practical computers, the task of managing and cross-referencing every important detail of the professional and social lives of so many interconnected, highly active agents was, in itself, a massive undertaking. The number of fake details and clean, reliable alibis that needed to be quickly produced without contradictions doubtless kept a sizable staff in Moscow Central awake for many long nights.

The magnitude of the challenge was multiplied every time the "UK Desk" in Moscow was purged by the Soviet Union. On at least one occasion, the entire Soviet espionage staff in London was recalled to Russia and liquidated. Every one of them. Imagine being a Soviet government employee and stepping over the warm bodies to have to pick up a complicated case like Burgess or Maclean in mid chapter. . . . Vodka anyone? . . . Better yet, who would like to be the financial auditor reporting to Moscow on the budget projections for these operations?

One of those lucky Soviets to inherit a position after the untimely purge of a boss that had also inherited *his* position after an untimely purge of *his* boss was Yuri Modin. Modin, born November 8, 1922, was a handler of the Cambridge Five from 1948

– 1951. We looked at those dates, paused, and double and triple checked them. After all, the role of a handler is somewhat paternalistic, and Yuri was substantially younger than his charges. However, that's what comes of killing off everyone with any experience, and the dates are correct to the best of our knowledge.

Modin managed to avoid being purged, himself, and arranged for the escape of two of the Cambridge Five to Russia, Guy Burgess and Donald Maclean. Modin, cagey bastard that he was, not only outlived the Soviet purges, but also outlived the Soviet Union. After the hammer and sickle were laid to rest, he spoke freely and extensively, though not necessarily truthfully, about his Cambridge charges. Modin finally died in Moscow, Russia, in 2007.

At least one other of what where doubtless several Cambridge Five handlers over the years was impacted by Stalin's purges. According to the Russians, Alexander Orlov was one of the handlers of the Cambridge Five from 1934 – 1938. Note we said "according to the Russians." That means maybe it's true, and maybe it's not. Truth is what Putin decides it is at any given moment. However, other Soviet defectors have corroborated the Orlov story.

Orlov, born Leiba Lazarevich Feldbin on August 21, 1895, in Babruysk, was a major in the Narodnyy Komissariat Vnutrennikh Del ("NKVD"), stationed in the Second Spanish Republic. He was best known for arranging the transport of the entire gold reserve of the Spanish Republic to the Soviet Union. In 1938, Stalin's "Great Purge," as opposed to all of Stalin's not-so-great purges reached Spain. A seasoned executioner, Orlov oversaw the "liquidation" of agents working for the NKVD in that country.

Then, in 1938, Orlov noticed his close friends and associates seemed to be disappearing at an alarming rate, scooped up for the torture and death portion of their service to the Soviet Union.

Suspecting he was next, Orlov escaped with his wife and children to the United States by way of Canada, where he defected to avoid being forcibly retired with a bullet. After the Soviet Union collapsed, Orlov claimed to have been deeply involved in the handling of the Cambridge Five. Though much of what Orlov said after he defected has been shown over the years to be fabrication, the Russians of today support his claims about the Cambridge Five and say he was, indeed, their handler from 1934 until 1938.

These purges not only caused problems for the Soviets, but also for historians who come along afterward, trying to figure out for certain who did what to whom and when. That's because purges tend to create a great deal of ass-covering activities by those who do not want themselves or their loved ones and relatives to be tortured and shot, and ass-covering activities result in highly inaccurate record keeping. Some reports are incomplete or inaccurate from the start, some are changed later by those who feel the need to cover their asses, and still more are changed by those who are bribed or who are protecting loved ones. As a result, it's likely that even the most enlightened, ethical Russian historians must pick through mazes of skillfully-placed misinformation. It's that much more difficult for outsiders. Nevertheless, being persistent or just plain stubborn, we do our best to wade through the contradictions, misunderstandings, and outright lies to piece together a picture of some of the most infamous traitors the United Kingdom has ever produced.

Some modern Western minds naturally want to organize the Cambridge traitors into the model of a single ring leader with followers, or they think of the spies in terms of "cells," like jihadis. That was not the case, even though at times Philby falsely believed he was a ring leader. The traitors were more of a network, and the Soviet Union was their leader. Some of the spies knew each other and plotted together at times, and some thought they were working alone. Many helped each other into positions that would better serve the Soviet Union. None of them regularly coordinated the others or issued the others orders. There was no command structure.

We believe Anthony Blunt was the most successful recruiter at Cambridge, but to be clear, he was *not* the handler of the recruits. He merely identified them and influenced them on behalf of the Soviets and turned them over to Soviet handlers from the Soviet intelligence service Obedinennoe Gossudarstvennoe Politicheskoe Upravleniye ("OGPU"), later the NKVD. Blunt was the hub of the Cambridge wheel, and so we start with him.

11

ANTHONY BLUNT

"THE FOURTH MAN"

ANTHONY FREDERICK BLUNT, KNOWN AS "THE FOURTH MAN," WAS likely the communist patient zero that infected the Cambridge population, turning many young people that might have gotten over their otherwise-innocent infatuation with Soviet ideals. If he wasn't actually patient zero, he was definitely the Soviets' first highly successful recruiter in that English elitist haven. Intelligent and self-serving, he seemed to be drawn to Soviet communism out of sheer ego and boredom. Cunning and discreet, he was the sort of man who could elicit conversations from people and then be forgotten by them. Fourth of the Cambridge Five to be discovered, we believe him to be the hub of the traitorous Cambridge wheel.

Anthony Frederick Blunt was born on September 26, 1907, in Bournemouth, Dorset, England, the third son of the Anglican Vicar Reverend Arthur Stanley Blunt and Hilda Violet Blunt. Anthony was a distant cousin of both King George V's wife, Queen Mary, and the Queen Mother Elizabeth, and the Blunt family visited Queen Elizabeth II and the Queen Mother several times prior to Elizabeth II's marriage to Lieutenant Philip Mountbatten.

Anthony Blunt grew up in a conservative family that was known to be anti-alcohol, anti-gambling, and pro-charity, and that maintained a pious reputation. The household was orderly, but sparse. When Anthony was four years old, the Reverend Blunt was assigned to the post of vicar of the British Embassy chapel in Paris. Blunt spent part of his childhood in that city.

The Reverend Blunt's appointment and tenure in that position might make a great historical comedy. The British Ambassador to France at the time, Lord Bertie of Thame—a name perfect for comedy—was proud of his vast collection of international pornography. He spent too little time on diplomacy and too much time involved in Parisian nightlife.

Wanting to set a better example than the ambassador, the Reverend Blunt announced that he and his wife intended to bring the British youth in France back to the straight and narrow by offering an alternative night life option. The Anglican Church was confident of Reverend Blunt's evangelical skills, and they honored his request to purchase a huge home in Paris for the purpose of entertaining up to five hundred wayward English souls at any one time.

We're not quite sure how one vicar and one vicar's wife could effectively corral five hundred young, drunken, Paris-loving British perverts at any one time, but we wish we had films of their attempts. Lord Bertie remained unconverted in spite of the Reverend Blunt's soirées, and the two men remained diplomatic, but distant. Lord Bertie had gone to great expense to acquire his world-class porn collection, and he was apparently in no mood to give it up.

Young Anthony apparently learned French quickly and became fluent. He also fell in love with art during his childhood years in France. We have no idea if the vicar managed to save any souls while in Paris, but Paris had a lasting impact on his young son, and, in time, he became one of England's greatest art historians.

After returning to England, Anthony attended Marlborough College. The Anglican Church had founded Marlborough as a safe and upright place to educate the children of the church's clergy. It's worth noting that in 1963, long after Anthony Blunt's graduation from the school, a group of graduates published a book exposing the pedophilic crimes of several staff members of the school. We do not know for certain whether young Anthony was one of their victims.

Blunt received a scholarship in mathematics to Trinity College at Cambridge in 1926. He studied mathematics and was apparently a gifted mathematician, but he decided to switch to foreign language and graduated with a first-class degree in Languages in 1930. He then became a French instructor and graduate fellow at Cambridge. While there, Anthony embraced another of his many talents—deception. He became a spy for the Soviet Union.

While at Cambridge, Blunt belonged to a secret society known as the "Apostles." His fellow Soviet spy, Guy Burgess, also became a part of the Apostles, and it may have been there that they developed a friendship. However they originally bonded, Burgess and Blunt then lived together in a home owned by Lord Rothschild. Blunt later described Burgess as charming and convincing. Blunt claimed that he and Burgess were never lovers, though they were both rather open about their homosexuality for a day and age when homosexuality was still severely punished by law.

In his memoirs, Blunt accuses Burgess of recruiting him to work for the Soviet Union. Holmes believes this claim is almost definitely false. Based on an overall assessment of the reports and documents available, as well as decades of experience working against the Soviets, Holmes believes Blunt was a quiet communist who was possibly working as a Soviet agent as early as 1928.

Another possibility was that Burgess *believed* he was recruiting Blunt, and Blunt had *already* been recruited. Some sources also believe that Blunt wasn't recruited until the late 1930s. That part is all rather foggy. However, it's fairly well-documented that Blunt recruited Maclean, Philby, and Cairncross of the Cambridge Five, as well as other Brits and the American traitor and magazine publisher Michael Whitney Straight.

Of all of the Cambridge Five, Blunt was the one most embarrassed by the damage to his personal reputation when his treason was made public. Perhaps in his mind, blaming Burgess for recruiting him somehow made him appear to be less guilty of his treason. There may have also been a much simpler motive for Guy Burgess and Anthony Blunt to keep the argument alive. Once the argument is settled, the next question becomes, "So who recruited Anthony Blunt?" Either the drunken chicken or the potentially drunken egg had to be spawned by someone else. There had to be an active recruiter at Cambridge prior to Blunt.

Blunt was talented, and he had talented cohorts, but their combined talents do not explain the number of Soviet spies in attendance at Cambridge by the time Guy Burgess showed up there in 1930. Whatever other political and moral sins Blunt might have committed, he was not the original sinner. It is not clear who the "first" Soviet spy at Cambridge was. He or she might remain forever unknown. Whoever it was, they found an excellent target in Blunt.

Then, in 1939, the Molotov-Ribbentrop Pact rocked Western communists' faith in the Soviet Union, including the Cambridge Five. The Molotov-Ribbentrop Pact was a pledge of non-aggression between the Soviet Union and Germany at a time when many young communists in the West were convinced that the Soviet Union would serve as a military and moral bulwark against the spread of militant fascism. The Pact secretly divided up Poland between the Soviet Union and Germany and allowed Germany to invade Poland without having to deal with a counter-attack by the massive Soviet Army. Lesser known secret agreements of the Pact also guaranteed that the Soviet Union would sell oil and war materials to Germany. If those Western communist enthusiasts had discovered that the Soviets had, for several years, been secretly operating training bases for Luftwaffe pilots and German army tank crews—both forbidden to Germany by the Treaty of Versailles—their shock and depression might have been even deeper.

Honoring the Pact, the Soviet Union stood by silent while the German Army invaded Poland. When the Luftwaffe destroyed the Polish Air Force with ease, and the German Army crushed the ill-equipped Polish Army, something besides freedom died on the plains of Poland. A Europe that, for the most part, had clung desperately to the sane, hopeful notions of diplomacy, cooperation, compromise, and peace found itself waking up from its nocturnal nightmares of the recent past to confront a new night-mare—WWII had begun. Europe's most cherished dream, its dream of "peace in our time," died on a muddy field in Poland under the bodies of young Polish soldiers. Hell had come to call again.

Like many young men and women of the United Kingdom, Anthony Blunt entered the British Army, and his language skills gained him an assignment to intelligence work with the British Expeditionary Force in France. It seems unlikely that Blunt was engaged in any important work in France. The French thought that the German Army could not break their vaunted Maginot Line. The German General Staff agreed.

While invading Holland and Belgium, the Germans avoided the Maginot Line and pushed their army through the Ardennes forest. They entered France at Sedan and drove on Paris before the French could redeploy enough troops and artillery to stop them. Blunt, along with most of the British Expeditionary Force, was squeezed into an area around Dunkirk and evacuated to England.

Back in England, Blunt was recruited to work for MI-5. Along with others of the Cambridge traitors, such as John Cairncross, Kim Philby, and Guy Burgess, Blunt quickly began to pass the Soviets deciphered intercepted German radio traffic. He also gave the Soviets useful information about German spy rings in Ukraine. The British intelligence services had excellent information on anti-Soviet spies in Estonia, Latvia, and Lithuania, and Blunt passed that information to the Soviets, as well. There are clues that Blunt was also involved in other tasks for the NKVD, but not enough information is available to completely define his espionage activities during WWII.

Near the end of the war, Anthony Blunt managed to ingratiate himself to the British Royal Family. At the request of King George VI, Blunt traveled to Germany and Italy and successfully retrieved letters that had been sent to Adolf Hitler, Nazi Foreign Minister Von Ribbentrop, Nazi Propaganda Minister Goebbels, and others by none other than the abdicated Royal Black Sheep, Edward, Duke of Windsor. The Nazis had entertained a fantasy about installing Edward as a puppet king of England after invading and conquering that country.

Whether or not the Duke of Windsor actively intended to cooperate with the Nazis, Edward was never going to be as useful to the Nazis as the Nazis thought he could be. The people of England were not going to rise up for Edward, nor would Edward have been the puppet leader of the Nazi government in the

United Kingdom. It was an overreach on the part of the Nazis to place much stock in him.

The Nazis actually attempted to hatch a plan to kidnap the Duke of Windsor and his American wife, Wallis Simpson, from Lisbon with the cooperation of Spanish Dictator Francisco Franco. Franco thought the plot was asinine, and we suspect that he warned the British, but that's a story for another day. The point is that, regardless of Edward's intentions or the feasibility of him rising to power with the Nazis, the letters could have been used as an effective propaganda tool against the British Royal Family and the British establishment overall at a time when the British social order was already under heavy attack.

Exactly how Blunt retrieved all of the letters is a bit of a mystery, though it seems he was able to do so due to his personal connections on the Continent. It certainly didn't hurt that those individuals who had the letters were, at the end of WWII, living in countries that were at the mercy of the Allies.

It's alleged by certain scholars and certain people in the diplomatic and intelligence communities that the letters included the Duke's expressions of faith in the Nazi party, and it is popularly thought that they contained highly-incriminating evidence about the Duke of Windsor's Nazi sympathies. Most British historians, specifically, believe that the letters were damning to the Duke, who was already an embarrassment to the United Kingdom.

That being said, keep in mind that the vast majority of people making claims about the content of these letters have never actually read the letters. We have also never read the text of the letters or any excerpts from them, nor do we personally know anyone who has. The letters may have been destroyed by the royal family, or they may be in some deep, dark vault with the rest of the royal family skeletons. We would make it clear that we do not know for certain what the letters say. Likely, the only ones who definitely knew the entire contents of the letters are Queen Elizabeth II and perhaps her royal corgis. . . . And Blunt.

It would have been a serious misstep on the part of Blunt if he did not read the letters before turning them over to the royal family. He made the claim in private circles that he had, but he never made the claim publicly or to the press. He kept that card up his sleeve, and by not playing it, he gave the British establishment good reason to keep its hands off him. It's worth noting that Anthony Blunt was never prosecuted for his treason.

After retrieving the letters, Blunt retired from MI-5 and accepted an appointment as the "Surveyor of the King's Pictures." Later, when King George VI died in 1953 and Queen Elizabeth II ascended the throne, Blunt was appointed "Surveyor of the Queen's Pictures." In that position, he was responsible for cataloging the monarch's art collection and ensuring its proper care.

In 1947, Blunt accepted a professor's chair as an art historian at London University, and he became the director of the prestigious Courtauld Institute of Art. Blunt wrote several important art history books and was an active teacher. According to those of his students who sat for interviews and answered press queries after Blunt was publicly identified as a Soviet spy, Blunt was a popular, enthusiastic professor and a skillful teacher. The honor roll of Blunt's students who rose to prominent positions in the art community in England includes renowned experts in several fields of art history.

According to employees who served under Blunt at the Courtauld, he was a kind and competent boss. Both his students and his employees expressed shock when they found out about Blunt's treachery. In the academic world and in the art community, Blunt was a paragon of intellect and reason.

Blunt's successful career in the art world does not mean that he stopped working for the Soviets. Though he no longer had direct access to communications inside of British intelligence or the British Foreign Office, he remained in frequent contact with Philby, Burgess, Maclean, Cairncross, and many other Soviet agents. Our belief is that Blunt had a high degree of trust from his Soviet handlers—for Soviet handlers, that is. The Soviets trusted no one. Not even themselves. However, Blunt was prudent, refined, and schooled in upper echelon behavior from a young age. He was not given to drinking as much as Philby, Burgess, and Maclean, and, according to testimony of some Soviets after the fall of the Soviet Union, as well as documents briefly opened at that time, the Soviets found Blunt generally more solid than the others. The Soviets used him to influence and encourage the rest of the Cambridge traitors.

By 1950, Blunt had been implicated by intercepted Soviet communications decrypted by the Venona project, by multiple defectors, and by British- and American-controlled agents. However, the wheels of investigation turned slowly. Blunt was no longer in a position to access sensitive information, and he was not the highest priority.

Viewers looking back on any counterintelligence operation are generally left with one or two impressions. It usually seems that the investigation moved "too slowly" and "they should have bagged the SOB sooner." Alternately, it occasionally seems that an investigation moved too quickly, and that too many loose ends were left untied before the investigation became known to the target or targets. We can always look back on MI-5's work or CIA's counterintelligence work and say if they moved too quickly or too slowly. We can also accurately predict the winner of every Kentucky Derby the day after the race is run.

Unfortunately for the investigators doing the thankless task of handling the investigation, they often don't even know precisely what's at stake when an investigation starts. On day one, they frequently don't know if it's a big fish, a little fish, a school of fish, a pod of killer whales or just another red herring. They also find themselves wading through a morass of skillfully-planted false leads from bogus defectors, fake doubles, planted fake messages transmitted by the target nation, and a colorful variety of other decoys. On top of all that, they are outnumbered and out-financed. They also don't want to accidentally destroy valuable work being done by loyal employees while they knock on doors and ask questions of a society of people who routinely answer questions from anyone outside their working team with warm, friendly responses such as, "Who the hell wants to know?"

Nonetheless, the wheels did continue to turn. After Burgess's and Maclean's defections to the Soviet Union in 1951, the temperature on Blunt's case file rose, and MI-5 skillfully grilled him. The interviews lasted hours.

The investigator always hopes to ask so many questions that the subject will have difficulty in not contradicting himself or offering a disprovable answer at some point in the interrogation. The interrogations were subtle and professional and did not include anything like sleep deprivation, physical abuse, scream-ing, or even withholding Blunt's tea and crumpets. Interrogations were repeated at odd intervals, months apart, and Blunt adroitly avoided tripping himself up. In the end, Blunt was foiled by an outsider, but until then, Blunt's public persona remained intact—so much so that the Queen knighted him in 1956.

In 1964, MI-5 investigator Arthur Martin discovered an old Cambridge acquaintance of Blunt's by the name of Michael Straight. Straight told Martin that Blunt had attempted to recruit him to work for the Soviets while he was at Cambridge. Investigators Arthur Martin and James Skardon approached Blunt with the new testimony and offered him immunity. They finally had him.

Some observers and historians question why Blunt was offered immunity once they had solid evidence on him. Perhaps it was done to get as much as they could from Blunt as quickly as possible. Blunt did not disappoint them. He spilled the beans and exposed over a dozen active Soviet agents.

In Holmes's view, jailing Blunt would not have been as valuable an outcome as exposing the other agents. It's certain that Blunt didn't tell his interrogators all the truth, but he told them a great deal of the truth. By exposing other agents, Blunt eliminated any future vacations behind the Iron Curtain.

Blunt, in fact, was at risk, even in the United Kingdom. The Soviets routinely assassinated defectors and turncoats, as well as, in Blunt's case, re-turned turncoats. Blunt was "free" and MI-5 kept the case under wraps, but Blunt could never be sure of his safety from the Soviets.

In November of 1979, Margaret Thatcher reported Blunt's treason while addressing the House of Commons. It has been suggested by Thatcherites (or are they Thatchonians?) that the Iron Lady did it to show the intelligence system that she was firmly in charge, not them. Maybe. But we should consider that Thatcher was aware that a book exposing Anthony Blunt, authored by Andrew Boyle, was on its way to bookshelves in the United Kingdom. Margaret Thatcher fans thought she had some higher political purposes in finally exposing Blunt. Our suspicion is that Thatcher had fairly good relations with the British intelligence services, and that she was just doing a little sensible damage control by beating the book to press.

After Blunt's exposure, he was "unknighted." We think we know what it looks like when a British sovereign knights someone. We wonder what the unknighting looked like. We have a few helpful suggestions if Her Majesty the Queen would like to hear them. If a man like Blunt is knighted with a sword, shouldn't he be unknighted with the same sword, or perhaps a disposable copy of it?

Once Maggie Thatcher wagged that long, angry finger in Blunt's direction, he was besieged by the press and by some not-very-adoring "fans." He had to travel incognito with guards. On one occasion during a drunken moment, apparently inspired by a Pink Panther film, Blunt hazarded a trip to the movies alone. Someone in the theater saw through his disguise and screamed out that he was there. Blunt had to beat a hasty retreat, one step ahead of a furious mob.

The Blunt case generated great conflicts within MI-5 and left some in MI-5 and MI-6 suspecting that Director General of MI-5 Sir Roger Hollis was a KGB agent. We'll just say Roger Hollis is a story for another cold, dark night.

Blunt died in 1983 without any assistance from the West or the Soviets. How can we be sure, you ask? Easy. By the time he died, the British intelligence community was enjoying watching him scurry about like an escaped fox, hounded by the Western press and angry British taxpayers. Killing him was more relief than they would have wanted to give him.

Blunt left behind memoirs that were not released to the public until 2009. In those memoirs, he explained that it was all a "big mistake," and that he was ever so sorry. Apparently, not all that sorry. However, the memoirs failed to answer pending questions about his recruitment by the Soviets and his post-WWII activities. The ugly little chicken that hatched this particularly traitorous egg remains unknown to this day.

12

GUY BURGESS

THE PLAYBOY

ANTHONY BLUNT ALWAYS CLAIMED HE WAS RECRUITED BY GUY Francis De Moncy Burgess, the second-most-infamous member of the Cambridge Five Soviet spy ring was. A renowned wealthy playboy, Burgess used his social status to work elite circles from the halls of the UK Parliament to MI-6, placing his fellow traitors in sensitive positions and providing the Soviets with reams of information that would be useful to them for decades.

Guy Burgess was born in Devonport, England on April 16, 1911. His father was Royal Navy Commander Malcolm Kingsford De Moncy Burgess. Guy loved the sea and expressed an interest in joining the Royal Navy from a tender age.

After attending Eton, he entered Dartmouth Naval College in January of 1925. However, Burgess left Dartmouth after only two years, supposedly because of inadequate eyesight. Apparently, that was an excuse that was conjured up to cover a scandal. It was alleged that Guy attempted to seduce a younger male student and was expelled for it. We are unable to verify the alleged scandal, but Burgess was never known to wear corrective eyeglasses during his adult life. After departing from Dartmouth Naval

College, Burgess returned to Eton, where he won academic prizes for his writing and his course work on history.

Burgess entered Trinity College at Cambridge in early 1930. By the end of that year, he had already completed the first part of the History Tripos, and in 1933, he gained a position as a graduate instructor. Staff members and prominent society members who met Burgess while he was at Cambridge remembered him as a brilliant academic, and many of his professors assumed that he would complete a doctorate and become a leader in his field. It was during this time at Cambridge that he developed close associations with fellow spies, Anthony Blunt and Kim Philby.

In 1934, Burgess, Philby, and Blunt went on what was described as a tourist trip to Moscow. While in Moscow, the Moscow police found Burgess passed out drunk on a park bench. According to the Moscow police, Burgess had in his possession letters of introduction to prominent Moscow professors from members of the Rothschild and Astor families. Whatever the real reason for the trip, Burgess was disappointed in Moscow. He apparently found the city depressing and dreary and voiced his disgust to his fellow Cambridge communists.

Upon his return from Moscow, the happy and confident communist Burgess denounced Soviet communism to anyone who would listen. He suddenly drifted to the right and became a born-again conservative. This was likely at the instructions of his Soviet controllers.

After leaving Cambridge, Burgess continued to use his academic connections, his wit, and his charm to develop more friendships in British society. While he rose in British social and political circles, he quickly developed a handicap—heavy drinking. Others of the Cambridge communists were able to leave their party habits behind when they graduated, but Burgess became even more wild and flamboyant than he had been in his college time.

In spite of his open, flamboyant homosexuality and his obvious alcoholism, politicians and other powerful members of society recognized Burgess's brilliance, and people in positions of power are often hungry for talented associates. Like many US congressmen and UK members of Parliament today, they weren't planning on doing the actual legislative work themselves, and they needed bright young people to make them look good. Burgess didn't need to be seen on the floor of Parliament. He just needed to produce intelligent-sounding positions on current events in the United Kingdom and Europe. He did that with a vengeance, and he became a valuable commodity to politicians and their masters.

Burgess became an assistant, a.k.a. the underpaid brain, to an influential right-wing conservative member of Parliament by the name of Captain (later Colonel) John Robert Jermain "Jack" Macnamara. Burgess accompanied Macnamara on a trip to Germany to meet Hitler, but he was unable to control his alcoholism on the trip. Macnamara fired him.

Burgess then traveled as a journalist in Spain during the Spanish Civil War, reporting on the Nationalists. When the Spanish Civil War broke out in 1936, he fed reports to the Soviet NKVD on a regular basis.

As WWII approached, British Prime Minister Neville Chamberlain used Burgess as a secret messenger to carry frantic, last minute appeals to French Prime Minister Édouard Daladier and Italian dictator Benito Mussolini. By the time the war started, Burgess was well placed amongst friends in MI-6. Like Kim Philby, Burgess was disgusted by the August 1939 Molotov-Ribbentrop Pact between the Soviets and Hitler, but apparently, he was not disgusted enough to stop working for the Soviet Union.

Burgess was assigned to D Section of MI-6, where he was responsible for recruiting suitable new agents for espionage and covert action in Europe. He accomplished two important services to the Soviet NKVD from his position in D Section. First, he helped insert active Soviet agents into MI-6, and second, he gave the NKVD an ongoing roll call of MI-6 agents.

Burgess provided the Soviets with a windfall of valuable intelligence at the beginning of WWII that remained useful to the NKVD for decades. After inserting Philby and other NKVD agents into critical positions within MI-6, Burgess took on the role of go-between. He resigned his MI-6 position. This basically changed his status to part-time "old boy club MI-6 crony," and allowed him more freedom to arrange communications with Soviet controllers and messengers.

When we speak of the MI-6 old boy club, we are referring to the unofficial network of upper-class British who were in or retired from MI-6. Most of them had grown up together, gone to the same schools, and married within their class. Most of MI-6 knew each other, or they knew the same people and, therefore, shared the same social credentials. As with all close communities in any country and culture, they gave each other the benefit of the doubt, and when troubles arose, they looked first at outsiders, such as Eric Roberts, the "untalented" bank clerk in a previous chapter. They looked last or not at all within their own ranks. It led to the mindset that only the lower classes would be disloyal. The Cambridge traitors took full advantage of that snobbery.

In 1944, Burgess joined the British Foreign Office and was given access to a broad array of diplomatic communications. When Burgess's old Cambridge pal, Hector McNeil, became Secretary of the Foreign Office, he hired Burgess as his top assistant.

Burgess routinely delivered top-secret documents to the Soviets from McNeil's office. McNeil was, and remained, highly impressed by Burgess's brilliance and thought himself lucky to be able to profit from Burgess's impressive skills. McNeil was confused, though, about who was using whom, and he was never able to admit that Burgess had duped him, even after Burgess escaped to Russia.

Burgess was assigned as Second Secretary to the British Embassy in Washington, DC, in 1947. His cohort, Kim Philby, was already there in the capacity of liaison to US intelligence services. At that time, Philby had not implicated their mutual pal Donald Maclean as a Soviet agent, even though Maclean had been under suspicion by MI-5 for several months thanks to Venona decryptions and the defections of several GRU and KGB agents to the West. By 1951, Maclean had been sent back to England and was about to be picked up for interrogation.

According to Burgess and Philby, they agreed that it was critical to get Maclean out of England as soon as possible. Of the three of them, Maclean was the most dedicated party line communist. Burgess and Philby always saw that as a sign of weakness in Maclean. Another weakness they recognized was Maclean's drinking problem and chronic depression. Because of this weak nature, they felt that Maclean's devout ideology would shatter like an empty vodka bottle smashed against the dark stone walls of the Kremlin once he was picked up by MI-5. It was something that had to be avoided.

Burgess and Philby decided together that Burgess would get a ticket home to warn Maclean. They chose to accomplish this by having Burgess simply be himself. Two things anyone could rely on with Burgess were that he would have sex with anyone who offered, and he would get drunk at any opportunity. Philby saw Burgess off on one of his on a wild and sodden adventures around Washington, DC, and within a few hours, Burgess had outraged several DC-area police departments. He was stopped three times in one day for speeding his Lincoln Continental convertible and for suspicion of drunk driving. Each time, he tore up the tickets and flaunted his diplomatic immunity.

The FBI had despised Burgess for a long time because of his frequent breaches of protocol and law, and Burgess was likely already under surveillance by their counterintelligence division. This was the last straw for the Bureau, and they demanded an official escalation by the US State Department. Within hours, the British ambassador happily rid himself of the diplomatic time bomb by sending Burgess home.

Burgess and Philby's mutual Cambridge cohort, Anthony Blunt, had received instructions for the extraction of Maclean from the United Kingdom, and Blunt delivered them to Burgess rather than expose himself by contacting Maclean directly. It is often alleged that Burgess was not supposed to accompany Maclean past France during his escape to Russia. The fact that the Soviets took the risk of waiting for Burgess's return to extract Maclean indicates that they were confident that Anthony Blunt, David Cairncross, and others had not yet been implicated, and that Burgess's cover was every bit as blown as Maclean's was.

In May of 1951, Burgess left behind his beloved hand-tailored wardrobe and several prized possessions and picked up Maclean. Just as Burgess had agreed with Philby that Maclean would talk fast if interrogated by MI-5, the NKVD likely viewed Burgess the same way. Burgess's heavy drinking and libertine behavior were a level of decadence that the Soviets saw as an indication of weakness and a failure of character. Also, the Soviets never assumed that the British would be any kinder to traitors in interrogations than the Soviets were, and that, therefore, a man like Burgess would certainly crack. Whether voluntarily or forcibly, and we do not know, Burgess joined Maclean in the escape at the last minute and boarded the ferry for France. Burgess's excuse was that Maclean was breaking down, and Burgess was afraid that Maclean would not make the escape on his own. Neither ever returned to England.

The CIA and the British intelligence services knew that the pair had escaped to Russia, but the agencies did not offer the public an explanation. From the public's point of view, Burgess and Maclean became "The Case of the Missing Diplomats." They were not seen again until they appeared on an interview for Soviet television in 1956.

When the story broke to the public, it broke in levels, as so often happens. The first explanation to the British public was that Burgess and Maclean had simply gone missing. Five years later, Burgess and Maclean appeared before reporters in Moscow and explained that they had never been involved in espionage, but had traveled to the Soviet Union to seek happiness in the communist paradise. For Burgess, any hope of paradise had likely been lost in a humiliating moment at Dartmouth when he was exposed as a homosexual and rejected by the British Naval establishment. We doubt that Burgess had known anything like happiness after that instance in his youth.

His time in Moscow would bring him no closer to happiness. Homosexuality was, and still is, unacceptable in the Soviet Union and was considered a capitalist "disease." Burgess was provided with an official state homosexual partner and all the vodka he could drink. He refused to learn Russian, and in his advanced state of alcoholism, he was useless as a prop to the Soviets.

Burgess tried on two occasions to get permission to visit England, but the United Kingdom never took his requests seriously. Even if the United Kingdom had approved, the Soviets would not have allowed him to embarrass them by Burgess returning to the

United Kingdom and then seeking asylum. In 1963, Burgess drank himself to death. Whether or not his impatient Soviet hosts assisted him with his permanent departure from the workers' paradise is unknown.

Guy Burgess's body was returned to England for burial in Hampshire with his mother. The one-time bon vivant and king of the Cambridge social jungle was missed by no one.

13

DONALD DUART MACLEAN

THE SINCERE ONE

DONALD DUART MACLEAN, THE MOST SINCERELY COMMUNIST OF the Cambridge Five, was also the first to be caught out as a spy for the Soviets. From his positions in the British Foreign Office, he kept Stalin apprised of US and UK political intentions on everything from the Nazi invasion of Russia, to the Allied commitment to West Berlin, and the West's reluctance to use nuclear weapons. Maclean helped Stalin determine just how far he could push the West.

Donald Maclean was born in London on May 25, 1913. His father was the distinguished liberal politician, Sir Donald Maclean. Sir Donald was admired and respected in the United Kingdom for his attempts to reduce child abuse and his sincere efforts to better the conditions of poor and working class people. Unfortunately, his sincerity passed down to his son, but not without getting twisted into treason along the way.

The younger Donald Maclean had a comfortable childhood and attended boarding schools that were identified with liberal philosophies. He spent five years at Gresham's School, which had produced several well-known socialist and communist writers and philosophers. In 1931, at age eighteen, he entered Trinity College at Cambridge, where he quickly gravitated toward like-minded youngsters such as Kim Philby, Anthony Blunt, and Guy Burgess.

By the time Maclean arrived at Cambridge in 1931, Blunt was already a graduate assistant and French instructor. Our personal best guess is that Blunt was well controlled by the Soviet NKVD before Maclean arrived at Cambridge. In fact, Blunt was likely waiting for Maclean's arrival, well-armed with information about Maclean and having plenty of cash with which to party. Maclean dove in head first.

After his long party at Cambridge was over, Maclean used his connections to obtain employment in the British Foreign Office. We know for certain from Soviet data that the Soviets fully controlled Maclean before his first day of work as a British government employee. From Soviet documents that were briefly exposed in the post-Soviet era, we also know that Maclean was first handled by a resident of the Soviet embassy operating under diplomatic cover. Maclean began producing valuable intelligence for the Soviet Union concerning the political intentions of the United Kingdom.

Shortly after, the Soviets left him "cold" for a while, or, in other words, inactive. Then they dispatched a skilled, reliable agent by the name of Kitty Harris. Harris had been born in London and later lived in Canada and the United States. Her travels and her personality made her well suited for deep cover work. Nothing about her except her Communist Party past in Canada would have caused alarm, and as a courier operating for the Soviets without diplomatic cover, she did not come under the routine scrutiny of MI-5. She simply appeared to be Maclean's lover. Eventually, she took on that role in reality.

Some say Kitty was Maclean's handler, as well, and some claim she was a cutout, but that's a bureaucratic argument. She was definitely on the team. Keep in mind that though we look for clean answers, some things are historically quite muddy, and it's difficult to assign everyone clear roles with complete accuracy. The times shortly before WWII were chaotic throughout Europe. The NKVD was also mired in its own confusion, which Stalin actively fueled to prevent too many people from teaming up against him, as he didn't want anyone being too powerful for too long. That resulted in more inner turmoil than was really convenient for Stalin, and it is now definitely inconvenient for historians.

From 1936 to 1938, Maclean produced large volumes of photos and documents from within the British Foreign Office. They were transmitted by a variety of sources, including coded messages that were decoded by the US Venona program. As a result, there was little that the British Foreign Minister knew that Moscow didn't know the next day. In retrospect, based on the variety and volume of information supplied by Maclean to his controllers, it now seems clear that Maclean was not working alone inside the Foreign Office in London.

In 1938, Maclean was assigned to the British Embassy in Paris. By this time, things were cooling off with Kitty. She was not regularly in Paris, and Maclean's handling was certainly shifted to a Paris team. While in Paris, he fell in love with Melinda Marling, the daughter of a wealthy American oil man. In 1940, as the German army was advancing through France, they married and fled to England.

Meanwhile, as Maclean was filling the Soviets' intelligence coffers with the United Kingdom's treasures, a former GRU officer named Walter Krivitsky had defected to France in 1937 and talked to the French security service. He then went to the United

States and testified before the Dies Committee, pre-cursor to the Un-American Activities Committee, in October of 1939. In January of 1940, Krivitsky sailed to London under a false name and was interviewed by Jane Archer of MI-5. Included in the information he gave MI-5 was that the Soviet Union had two agents employed in the British Foreign Office, and that an English journalist had spied for the NKVD in Spain. He also gave MI-5 descriptions of approximately sixty-five Soviet agents working in the British Foreign Office and British intelligence services. Maclean was vaguely implicated by Krivitsky's descriptions.

The following year on February 10, 1941, Krivitsky was murdered by Soviet intelligence in the Bellevue Hotel in Washington, DC. He was found with a .38 revolver in his hand with one chamber fired and one shot in the head. It was recorded as a suicide by the local police, who didn't know to look any closer. We know now from files temporarily opened at the end of the Soviet Union and before the Putin dictatorship that Krivitsky was murdered by the Soviets.

Unfortunately, the magnitude of Krivitsky's information was so great that MI-5 concluded he must have been planted by the NKVD in an attempt to ignite a purge of British intelligence services. On the surface, this might seem like sloppy work by MI-5, but MI-5 was relying on Krivitsky's memory and little documentation. Krivitsky had escaped to Paris on the lam from the NKVD in 1938, ahead of one of Stalin's purges of Soviet intelligence staff in Europe. The Soviets anticipated that Krivitsky would certainly inform the UK government, and they took great pains to plant decoy information, thus successfully making Krivitsky look like he was still working as their agent.

When judging MI-5's response to Krivitsky in 1940, we must also take into account that for twenty years, MI-5 had been constantly barraged by false information from Soviet provocateurs in the form of fake defectors and doubles. Had MI-5 and Scotland Yard believed half of the sensational "revelations" they received, there might have been too few government employees left out of jail for the British government to function at all.

While uncertainty plagued MI-5 and other Western counterintelligence operations, the Soviets suffered from similar doubts. One of the NKVD's case handlers for Maclean and Philby was Elena Modrzhinskaya. Elena was a cliché Soviet female NKVD analyst who resembled the fictional Colonel Rosa Klebb of James Bond fame. From her, we gain a valuable insight into the Stalinist mindset.

Elena was convinced that Maclean, Philby, and their cohorts were withholding information about the identities of British SOE agents sent to sabotage Russia. It was beyond Soviet conception that there were no such British saboteurs working against the Russians while they were allied with the West during WWII. She also thought that the windfall of intelligence from Maclean, Philby, Burgess, et al., was just too good to be true. Living in the Soviet police state without first-hand experience in the United Kingdom, Elena was not capable of understanding how so much critical, secret information could so easily slip out of England. At times, this doubt caused the Soviets to lose some of the value of the information sent by the Cambridge traitors.

One of the more famous instances of the Soviet Union ignoring valuable intelligence from Maclean and others of the Cambridge Five was when both they and the United Kingdom warned the Soviet Union of the impending German attack in June, 1941. Stalin insisted that the Soviets should not mobilize defenses against a German invasion. That failure to trust his information cost Russia millions of casualties and nearly allowed the Germans to defeat the Soviet Army *en totem*. When the German

Army was simultaneously knocking at the gates of Moscow, Leningrad, and Stalingrad, Stalin realized that his spies in England had been right. After that, he placed more credence on the intelligence received from the Cambridge Five. (See *Spycraft: Critical Moments in Espionage*.)

Another bit of valuable information that Maclean passed to Moscow during WWII was a complete copy of the minutes of British Cabinet Committee meetings concerning the development of atomic weapons by the United Kingdom and the United States. Moscow had several other sources of technical intelligence on atomic weapons development, but Maclean's information gave Stalin a precise reading on the long-term intentions of the United Kingdom and the United States.

By 1942, Maclean's friends and associates noticed an increase in Maclean's drinking. Since his graduation from Cambridge, he had developed a reputation as a reliable and stable individual. Previously, his drinking and social conduct at parties was controlled, but around this time, he became more boisterous and argumentative. While increased drinking and a personality change would often catch the attention of counterintelligence watchdogs today, during WWII, heavy drinking and a lack of social restraint would not have been quite as noticeable.

In 1944, the Soviet Union hit the jackpot again when Maclean was assigned to the British Embassy in Washington, DC. During his time in DC, Maclean did his most valuable work for the Soviets. He effected to be assigned to the British team in any US/UK atomic policy meetings. As a result, Stalin remained well-informed about US and British nuclear planning and policies.

After WWII, Germany was divided into four temporary occupation zones controlled by France, the United Kingdom, the United States, and the Soviet Union. The German capital city of Berlin was within the Soviet sector, but it was subdivided between the four occupying nations. The Soviet Union had agreed that France, the United Kingdom, and the United States would have unhindered access to road, railroad, and air corridor routes to West Berlin.

Thanks in large part to intelligence gathered by Donald Maclean, Stalin knew that the Western powers would not engage in a shooting war with the Soviet Union to keep control of West Berlin. As a result, on June 24, 1948, the Soviets broke their treaty with the Allied nations by blockading the land routes to West Berlin, calculating that the Western powers would be forced to abandon the city. At the same time, the United Kingdom and the United States were able to safely predict that Stalin would not attempt to shoot down Allied aircraft flying to Berlin. The United Kingdom and the United States combined efforts in a massive airlift to keep Berlin supplied. It was an expensive and risky undertaking, and the Soviets were certain that the West could not succeed.... It did.

Between June of 1948 and May of 1949, at the cost of 101 casualties, the Western powers flew an astonishing 2.3 million tons of supplies to West Berlin. The Soviets finally lifted the blockade on May 12, 1949. The long-term effects of the Soviet antagonism were to draw the people of West Germany closer to the Western Allies and to foster overwhelming support in the West for the North Atlantic Treaty Organization ("NATO") as a bulwark against Soviet aggression.

Maclean was reassigned to Cairo in 1948. In Cairo, he wrote to his Soviet masters and asked that he be allowed to come "work in Russia," and that his wife, Melinda, was "perfectly prepared to go." His request was denied. Holmes suspects that was because Maclean would have been of no use to the Soviets in Russia, but he was still of some use to them in the British Foreign Office.

While in Cairo, Maclean's drinking increased and his social restraint decreased. His drunken orgies involved him in scandals, and the British Foreign Office recalled him to London. Rather than fire him, in 1950, Maclean was assigned as head of the American Department in the British Foreign Office in London.

North Korea invaded South Korea without prior permission from their Soviet allies in June of 1950. At that point, Stalin had to decide whether to encourage North Korea to accept a peace agreement, or to support them in a war against the West. Some historians and analysts today believe that Stalin's decision to back North Korea was based in large part on the intelligence provided by Donald Maclean—intelligence that the United States and its allies did not intend to allow the Korean conflict to escalate to a nuclear war, and that the United States did not intend to directly attack China or the Soviet Union. Stalin knew just how far he could push.

By 1951, the evidence against Maclean was undeniable. Newer leaders were rising in MI-5, MI-6, and the Foreign Office. The "old boy" stranglehold on these institutions was broken, in large part by the hard-working, well-educated middle class professionals of both genders who had joined the expanded operations during the crisis of WWII. Their lack of pedigrees left them unimpressed with class distinctions and unafraid to challenge the old establishment. Without his social privilege protecting him from scrutiny, Maclean was done.

Ironically, the very sort of social revolution that Maclean had aspired to work for in the Soviet Union had occurred under his nose in British government. That institutional change in MI-5 selected out the best of both the experienced "old blood" and the enthusiastic "new blood" to forge a far more efficient and effective organization that made the activities of men like Maclean and Philby much more difficult to hide.

In May of 1951, a few days before Maclean was to be picked up by MI-5, he escaped to the Soviet Union at the behest of Kim Philby and Anthony Blunt. Guy Burgess drove Maclean to Southampton, where the two of them boarded a ferry for France. (See chapter on Guy Burgess.)

Maclean adapted well to his ungilded cage in Moscow, living in the communist paradise that he had always wanted. He studied Russian, had his name put on a book about British foreign policy, and worked for the Institute of World Economics and International Relations. He maintained a loyal Communist Party line, apparently more comfortable in his modest, highly-regulated Soviet life than his fellow traitors ever were.

Maclean's wife, Melinda, played the innocent, and she is popularly portrayed that way in fictional accounts of the Cambridge traitors. However, Holmes believes she was far from a clueless victim, and that at a minimum, Melinda knew Maclean was spying for the Soviets and actively helped cover for him. For example, when Maclean was stationed in DC, Melinda, pregnant with one of their children, chose an obstetrician in New York City, several hours away from their home before puddle-jumper flights or the Interstate Highway System. This gave Maclean regular cover to go to New York City. Not only is this a nonsensical choice for any pregnant woman, but from Venona decryptions, we know that the Soviets were aware of these appointments and communicated them in coded messages. Also, her quotes and behaviors over the years were overall consistent with those of a woman who was keeping a secret for her husband.

Melinda voluntarily joined Maclean in Moscow in 1952. According to Kim Philby's granddaughter, Charlotte Philby, as well as other sources, Philby left his third wife to be with Melinda Marling Maclean in 1965. Apparently, Philby thought that communist communal property thing applied to wives, too.

To reward Maclean for his good behavior, the KGB made him a colonel, but only in nominal terms. He had no authority or responsibility in the Soviet spy organization. Maclean lived another thirty-three years in his Moscow reality until his death in 1983. By this time, Melinda was living in the United States, and his children were in England. Maclean's ashes were sent back to England to be buried with those of his parents at Trinity Church, Penn, Buckinghamshire.

14

KIM PHILBY

THE MAN WHO CAUSED A THOUSAND DEATHS

THE MOST INFAMOUS MEMBER OF THE CAMBRIDGE FIVE WAS Harold Adrian Russell "Kim" Philby. Of all the Cambridge traitors, Philby achieved the greatest damage to Western nations and their intelligence services. His betrayals were directly responsible for the deaths of numerous British intelligence personnel and assets, several hundred Polish and Ukrainian insurgents, and several hundred anti-communist Armenians. Frequently called "The Third Man," he was the third of the Cambridge Five dirtbags to be caught.

Kim Philby was born in Punjab, India in 1912. The nickname Kim came from the Rudyard Kipling adventure espionage novel. Kim's father, H. Saint John Philby, was a brilliant, but not altogether conventional, British diplomat, as well as a socialist and a member of the British intelligence service.

While T. E. Lawrence, a.k.a. Lawrence of Arabia, was organizing the Hashemite Arabs against the Turks in Arabia during WWI, Saint John Philby was organizing the Hashemites' Arab opponent, Ibn Saud. With the help of the senior Philby, Ibn Saud defeated the Hashemites and founded Saudi Arabia. Saint John

Philby spent much of his life in the Arabian peninsula and converted to Islam in 1930, likely for political reasons to continue to work more easily with the Saudis, as the Wahabbist influence on the royal house was increasing. Then, in 1945, at the age of sixty, he bought a sixteen-year-old Arab wife at a slave market at Taif. One might say he truly embraced his work.

In a sense, Saint John Philby also betrayed England. Not only was he in unauthorized correspondence with Ibn Saud, but also, when Ibn Saud was willing to ink a deal with British oil investors, Saint John Philby sought bids from American companies. Ibn Saud ended up granting American oil companies a sixty-year exclusive license for oil exploration in the rich fields of eastern Saudi Arabia.

In 1928, Kim Philby qualified for an academic scholarship, and at the age of sixteen, he entered Trinity College at Cambridge. He completed majors in both Economics and History, and he graduated with honors. While at Cambridge, Philby joined a socialist political group, and he worked in campaigns for local Labor Party candidates. Though it's never been proven, we believe that he was approached during that time by the Soviet OGPU.

The precise details of Philby's recruitment are unknown. Philby claimed in his memoirs that his first wife, Litzi Friedmann, recruited him in Vienna, but the evidence doesn't support that claim. Philby was likely well-controlled by the Soviets before he ever met Litzi in Vienna in 1933. Also, Philby's memoirs were published from inside the Soviet Union and were fine tuned to serve as propaganda misinformation to anyone willing to believe anything that Philby had to say at that point in his life.

Philby married Litzi to prevent her being arrested for her Communist Party of Austria activities, and the couple returned to England in 1934. They soon parted ways on friendly terms, but they remained married until 1946. Their eventual break up may have been a product of their work for the Soviets. It may also have been influenced by the fact that Philby had fathered three children with Aileen Furse while married to Litzi. Philby married Aileen one week after his divorce and proceeded to have two more children with her. But now back to the real story . . .

During the Spanish Civil War in 1937, Philby traveled to Spain undercover as a somewhat anti-communist journalist. He was in the employ of the British Secret Service, but he was actually a double agent working for the NKVD. While there, Philby was welcomed by the Nationalists, and he wrote articles sympathetic to General Franco's Nationalist forces.

In Philby's travels in Spain, a car he was riding in suffered a near miss by an artillery shell fired by Republican forces. His three travel companions were killed, and he was mildly wounded. With so many English volunteers fighting on the side of the socialist Republicans, Franco was anxious to find a pro-Nationalist Englishman. Franco quickly decorated Philby as a war hero, apparently for sitting in the right car seat at the right time. This decoration from Franco helped establish Philby as an anti-communist champion, and he gained even more access to important people in Spain.

Both the British and the Soviets had tasked Philby with finding out as much as he could about the German Panzer Mk1 and Panzer Mk2 tanks being used by the Nationalist army. They also wanted information about the highly-advanced German Messerschmidt Bf 109 fighter being introduced into the German Condor legion, which was flying for Nationalist Spain.

Even at this early stage in his career as a double agent, the Soviets demonstrated a high opinion of Philby's ability and loyalty to the Soviet Union. Remarkably, the NKVD trusted Philby with the sensitive task of organizing the assassination of General Franco. However, Philby was surrounded by loyal Nationalists and would have needed adequate assets from outside of the Nationalist camp in order to achieve that goal. From the scant information now available, though, it seems the NKVD never provided those minimal requirements in manpower for Philby to lead an assassination attempt on the Spanish leader.

As we mention in the chapter on Donald Duart Maclean, a Soviet defector by the name of Walter Krivitsky told MI-5 in January of 1940 that the Soviet Union had two agents employed in the British Foreign Office, and that an English journalist had spied for the NKVD in Spain. Philby's career might have ended right there if Krivitsky's information had been acted on with alacrity, but MI-5 either doubted Krivitsky or failed to make the connection to Philby. Several of the English journalists working in Spain during the Spanish Civil War had communist leanings, and this may have created enough of a smoke screen to shelter Philby from suspicion.

In July of 1939, a few months after the Nationalists won the Spanish Civil War, Kim Philby returned to England. A month later, he was confronted with ethical and intellectual challenges to his loyalty to the Soviet Union.

In the 1930s, many of Europe's communists based their faith in communism on the childish notion that only the Soviet Union could stop what seemed to them like the inexorable growth of fascism. One critical element in maintaining a "Stalin will save us" philosophy was ignorance of the fact that Stalin was far more fascist than most fascists.

Many of Europe's and America's true believers in communism maintained their political faith by denying the growing body of evidence that indicated the Soviet workers' paradise had become a workers' hell. It was common for European communists to blame the European and American establishment for spreading propaganda against communists. The fact that many anti-communists were, at times, willing to disregard facts when discussing communism or the Soviet Union only led to a deeper faith on the part of the devout communists.

In August of 1939, Europe was hastening toward war. British Prime Minister Neville Chamberlain attempted to buy "peace in our time." He traveled to Germany to meet Hitler. Chamberlain and Hitler signed an agreement that Hitler would not invade any more countries in exchange for Britain accepting German occupation of western Czechoslovakia. Czechoslovakia was not consulted about the agreement.

Hitler had no intention of keeping his agreement. However, to some Europeans, it seemed that Hitler's perceived reluctance to engage in a two-front war would prevent the Germans from attacking westward into Belgium or France. Then, when Moscow and Berlin proudly announced the Molotov-Ribbentrop Pact for non-aggression in late August, many previously devout members of the communist faith decided it was time to find a new religion. Many of them did.

According to witnesses, Philby was among those most stunned by the pact between Stalin and Hitler. Philby probably had rationalized his betrayal of the nation that had treated him so well with the standard "rich boy communist" notion that communism was preventing the spread of fascism and world war. The realization that Stalin and the Soviet Union had done so much to create the coming war must have been devastating for most European communists. By now, Philby had to realize that there was nothing ideal about the Soviet communist reality.

It appears that Philby might have decided that his life as a double agent was over, but the NKVD was not accepting resignations. Philby failed to show up to scheduled contacts and did not communicate with his Soviet controllers for several months. He went to France to cover the war and apparently had no contact with the Soviets during this period. In May of 1940, as France was on the verge of defeat by the German Army, the United Kingdom quickly evacuated its expeditionary force. Philby returned to England.

He was soon assigned to the training staff of Britain's Special Operations Executive. Winston Churchill told the SOE to "set Nazi-occupied Europe ablaze." Unfortunately, the conflagrations envisioned by Churchill and his staff never amounted to more than a smoldering campfire.

The Abwher, which was the German military intelligence and counterintelligence organization, had penetrated the SOE. The Germans succeeded in doubling enough of the agents sent by the British to maintain direct communication with the SOE and read the orders to agents in the field as they were transmitted. While the Gestapo was always quick to claim credit for rounding up so many of the agents and infiltrators sent into Nazi-occupied Europe, it was the German military that scored so many coups against the British SOE.

During this early stage of the war, the Soviets re-established control of Philby. The precise details of Philby's reactivation by agents of the NKVD, are not known, but it clearly occurred prior to Hitler's invasion of Russia in June, 1941. In fact, thanks to British code breaking successes, Philby was able to warn the Soviets of Hitler's plan to invade Russia.

The NKVD understandably doubted Philby's reliability. Philby had probably unwittingly expressed his doubts about Stalin and the Soviet Union to social contacts who were reporting his activities to their own NKVD controllers. Nonetheless, the warning of the coming German invasion of Russia had been duplicated by other independent sources, and the British government directly warned the Soviet Union about German intentions and troop build-ups in the East. However, Stalin remained mistakenly convinced that the information was an attempt by the British government to manipulate the Soviet Union into a war with Germany.

Philby's warnings were wasted. Stalin did not order the massive Soviet Army to defensive positions in Poland and Russia. However, when Philby was proven right, Moscow regained substantial confidence in him. At the same time, when the Germans made such swift gains in Russia, Stalin was left embarrassed with his own senior intelligence staff officers.

To say that Moscow trusted Philby would be inaccurate. Stalin trusted no one. Even the high-level henchmen that Stalin relied on to organize the massive purges of the 1930s invariably ended up dead themselves. For Moscow, it was a question of deciding how much credence to place on Philby's information.

The chief Soviet analyst assigned to handle information from Philby and his associates at this point in time was Elena Modrzhinskaya. As we mentioned in the chapter on Maclean, the idea that Philby and the rest of the Cambridge Five could operate so freely in wartime Britain seemed unbelievable to Soviets accustomed to life in Stalinist Russia. Elena assumed that Philby and the rest of the Cambridge Five were all "triple" agents posing as double agents. However, the weight of valuable and accurate information that the five were able to provide soon convinced her superiors that Philby and his cohorts were, in fact, good sources.

As Philby continued his service to the Soviets, he maintained good cover by working hard against the Germans for both MI-5 and MI-6. Philby was promoted to a position with Allied agents who were providing the United Kingdom with information from Spain and Portugal.

In late 1942, a brilliant young American counterintelligence specialist named James Jesus Angleton passed Kim Philby information about a British-controlled agent who had been captured by the Gestapo and executed. Philby was accustomed to being one of the smartest people in any crowd, but in Angleton, he had met his intellectual superior.

To Angleton, something about Philby seemed insincere, so he checked Philby's response to the information about the executed agent via another member of MI-5 and discovered that Philby did not report the execution to his superiors in London. Angleton warned MI-5, but his warning fell on deaf ears. The intelligence community in London prior to, during, and for many years after WWII, suffered from a debilitating case of institutional overconfidence. The majority of the British intelligence community thought that nothing of any use could come from an "American cowboy," and they ignored Angleton's repeated warnings over the years.

With the threat from the Axis powers gone after the 1945 defeat of Germany, Philby continued to serve his masters in Moscow. In August of that year, Konstantin Volkov, a Russian NKVD supervisor in Istanbul, Turkey, contacted British MI-6 and offered to defect to the West. Volkov requested a large payment in exchange for the names of two NKVD agents working in the British Foreign Office, which he would deliver in person. The Foreign Office did not know it at the time, but the names Volkov would have delivered were Guy Burgess and Donald Maclean, and one man working with MI-5—Kim Philby. The British were happy to meet Volkov's price.

Unfortunately, MI-5 dispatched Philby to Istanbul to personally oversee the extraction of Volkov and his family. Philby immediately informed his Soviet controller and delayed his travels, avoiding showing up in Istanbul for three weeks. How Philby was allowed to delay his travel to Istanbul that long in the midst of such an important assignment without being suspected of duplicity remains a mystery.

Naturally, Volkov and his family were promptly returned to Moscow under guard. As near as we can tell, after a long and unpleasant interrogation, the Soviets burned Volkov to death by inserting him slowly into a furnace. This was, and for a long time remained, a popular method of execution for captured Russian traitors.

In 1947, Philby was promoted to head of British intelligence in Turkey. Turkey might seem to have been an inglorious assignment, but Turkey bordered on the Soviet Union, and it was on the front line of the Cold War as a staging base for infiltrators into the Ukraine and other Soviet occupied areas, including what was, at the time, the Soviet satellite state of Albania.

During WWII, the United Kingdom had financed and armed Enver Hoxha and his communist guerrillas in Albania. The British assisted the group in infiltrating Axis-occupied Albania with great success. However, once the war was over, Hoxha established a ruthless communist police state in Albania. At that point, the United Kingdom, her allies, and thousands of exiled Albanians wanted Hoxha and his ruthless thugs removed from that country.

The British were seen by the United States as experts in Albania because of their long experience there, which pre-dated WWI. The United States was happy to finance the training of Albanian exiles and let the United Kingdom control the operation. Unfortunately, Kim Philby was placed in charge of having Albanian freedom fighters infiltrated into Albania.

The program was quite successful until Philby took control. Once he did, anti-communist Albanians were quickly rounded up and executed, and the program failed. We do not know the precise number of betrayed Albanians that were sent to their deaths, but based on the available evidence, it seems that several hundred Albanians lost their lives as a result of Philby's betrayal.

In September of 1949, Philby went to Washington, DC, to serve as the United Kingdom's chief intelligence representative to the United States at the UK Embassy. His position allowed him access to Top Secret messages between the United States and the United Kingdom, and he was able to provide the Soviets with a gold mine of information. James Angleton was one of Philby's primary contacts in Washington. Angleton maintained cordial relations with Philby, but he remained suspicious of the Englishman.

Philby was now at the pinnacle of his career as a Soviet agent, and he kept Moscow abreast of key US and British communications. He had access to information about joint British and US assistance to anti-communist insurgents in Poland and the Ukraine. As a result, several hundred more insurgents were rounded up and executed. But Philby's time was running out.

The US National Security Agency ("NSA"), in cooperation with the United Kingdom and Australia, was running a project known as "Venona." The project, which had been started by the US Army Signal Corps shortly before WWII, worked on deciphering captured Soviet signals communications. Fortunately for the NSA, the Soviets had made critical errors in the preparation of some of their daily code ciphers. Someone producing the ciphers had gotten lazy and started reusing old code ciphers to save time and effort in randomizing new ciphers.

This blunder violated one of the cardinal rules of communications security—never use the same system-wide cipher for more than a day, and never use the same one-time cipher more than once. It creates an extra volume of material with the same cipher, and the messages refer to an increasing number of known events over a longer window of time. This makes it much easier for a skilled team to break the cipher.

Thanks to Venona, the British were warned about a spy in their embassy in Washington, DC, who was traveling to New York on a regular schedule to meet his Soviet controller. Philby learned of the spy from his superiors, and he was tasked with ferreting out the mole. As soon as Philby was briefed, he knew that the mole in question had to be his Cambridge cohort, Donald Maclean. Philby pretended to investigate.

In October of 1950, while Philby was continuing with his farcical investigation to find a mole in the UK Embassy, his other Cambridge cohort, Guy Burgess, was also posted to the British Foreign Office in Washington, DC, where he had been coming and going for the past three years. Philby likely would have preferred that the heavy-drinking, obnoxious Burgess not show up in Washington again just then, but Philby knew better than to leave Burgess to his own devices. Burgess actually lived as a guest with Philby and his second wife, Aileen. The arrangement made it easier for Philby to keep tabs on the reckless Burgess, but it also closely linked him to Burgess.

Burgess quickly ran afoul of the US State Department and the Federal Bureau of Investigation ("FBI"). He acted as a one-man diplomacy wrecking ball, routinely driving UK Embassy vehicles on drunken adventures around the DC area. In one unverified anecdotal report, Burgess approached an FBI agent who may have been tailing him and offered the man sexual favors. J. Edgar Hoover was already suspicious of Burgess and angry at his conduct. The FBI agent that Burgess propositioned assumed that Burgess's real intention was not to seduce him, but to insult the FBI. From Hoover's point of view, Burgess had openly declared his contempt for the FBI and the US government.

In the meantime, Maclean was sent back to London from his station in Cairo. Philby and Burgess decided that Burgess would return to England to warn Maclean that he would soon be taken in for interrogation by MI-5. In May of 1951, Burgess and Maclean escaped through France to the Soviet Union. (See chapter on Guy Burgess.)

Because Philby's close association with Burgess was well known in both DC and London, Philby finally fell under suspicion. He was questioned multiple times, and for a while, he managed to avoid confirming suspicions. However, besides the mounting evidence, Philby was in trouble for another reason. MI-5 and MI-6 were both changing. Many of the wartime newcomers to British intelligence were from outside of the traditional "old boys club" of the British elite. The new breed of serious, less connected, less arrogant, and more dedicated intelligence professionals were influencing the culture in the British intelligence community, and being a good old boy was no longer an adequate alibi.

Philby's case could not be proven in court without burning valuable assets that the British had acquired from within the Soviet government, so Philby was quietly shunted aside, isolated from sensitive information, and forced out of MI-6. He took up a full time job as a journalist. Moscow Central assumed that Philby was under full time surveillance and was being dangled as bait to help capture his controller. The Soviets apparently decided to break off contact with Philby.

Members of Parliament remained loudly concerned about possible Soviet moles, and they routinely demanded "action." In 1955, British Foreign Secretary Harold McMillan reported to Parliament that Kim Philby had been cleared of any wrongdoing. This was, of course, complete and utter nonsense, but it momentarily quieted the Parliament and the press.

Philby moved to Lebanon and lived with his father, Saint John Philby, and Saint John's second family for a while, working as a correspondent for *The Economist* and *The Observer*. Saint John Philby's high-level contacts in Jordan, Saudi Arabia, Yemen, and the Gulf States likely made Philby a more valuable correspondent for his employers. Those contacts would have also made Philby valuable to the organization now being called the KGB.

In addition to spying for the Soviets, Philby busied himself in Beirut by seducing Eleanor Brewer, the wife of *New York Times* correspondent Sam Brewer. Philby's second wife, Aileen, died in England in December of 1957. Eleanor Brewer obtained a divorce from Sam and married Philby on January 24, 1959.

In 1961, Soviet KGB Major Anatoliy Mikhaylovich Golitsyn defected to the United States with his family from Helsinki, Finland. James Jesus Angleton had by then risen to the position of Director of Counterintelligence at the CIA, and he personally interviewed Golitsyn upon his arrival in the United States. Golitsyn brought with him more evidence against Philby. MI-5 now felt that it had sufficient exposable evidence with which to prosecute the traitor.

Philby's wife, Eleanor, noted in 1962 that Philby's heavy drinking became worse, and that he suffered from episodes of severe depression. It could be that Philby was informed by a Soviet operative that Golitsyn would expose him, or Philby may have simply assumed that Golitsyn or other defectors were bound to do so. Late that year, MI-6 dispatched an experienced officer by the name of Nicholas Elliot to Beirut to offer Philby a return to England and protection from prosecution in exchange for Philby's cooperation. When Elliot arrived, he found Philby "too drunk to stand up." Philby at first denied the obvious, but then he agreed to take the deal and to meet with Elliot in a sober state to arrange for his travel to England.

On January 23, 1963, Philby failed to show up at a party where he was supposed to meet his wife. Later, Philby claimed that he departed on a Soviet freighter for Russia. Other theories have been presented, including an overland trip through Syria and Iraq.

It is possible that the Soviets placed surveillance on Philby once Golitsyn defected. It is also possible that Philby was already acting as an agent of opportunity for the Soviets in the Middle East, and that he was in routine contact with a Soviet controller. It may be that Elliot had been observed approaching Philby, and that the KGB decided to invite Philby for a visit to Moscow with or without his cooperation. Philby knew MI-6 and MI-5 well enough to know that they would keep their word, and that he would live comfortably in England. It would seem that, at that point in his life, Philby would have had more dread of traveling to Moscow than he would have had for life in England under immunity.

The suggestion has been made that Philby actually returned to Moscow to act as a "double of a double" for MI-6. Holmes finds that highly unlikely. Well, let us be frank. Holmes finds the suggestion silly. By that time, no one in British intelligence trusted Philby, and like every other person in Russia, Philby had the trust of no one in Soviet government. Even if the British had been willing to try to use Philby from inside of Russia, they would have understood that Philby would have no freedom of movement and no opportunity to operate against the Soviets from within that country.

On July 30, 1963, the Soviet Union announced that Philby had been granted Soviet citizenship. Many in the West have expressed frustration that Philby was allowed to escape rather than face prosecution. Given the conditions in the Soviet Union in 1963, we think that being granted Soviet citizenship constituted a far grimmer imprisonment than the West would have inflicted on the traitor.

In Russia, Philby was given a small apartment—a lavish residence by Soviet standards—and Eleanor joined him in September of 1963. Philby was kept under guard. The Soviets explained that this was to protect him, even though they and Philby knew that there would be no assassination attempt made against him by the West. He spent his time producing a memoir that no one took too seriously, including the KGB employees who wrote it for him.

According to some sources, while Eleanor was away in the United States to renew her passport, Philby seduced his friend and fellow traitor Donald Maclean's wife, Melinda Marling. Eleanor found out about the affair and left both Philby and Moscow in May of 1965.

Philby subsequently married his fourth wife, Rufina Ivanova, in 1972. According to Rufina, Philby drank heavily. She also said he attempted suicide a few times, but that the guards always caught him before he could make his permanent departure from his Soviet Workers' Paradise.

In 1988, Kim Philby finally did something that made both the Soviet Union and Western governments happy. He died of a heart attack. Since he was permanently safely beyond the reach of reporters and other inquirers, the Soviet Union transferred Philby to the "Dead Heroes" division of the KGB. The KGB gave Philby's carcass several cute red medals with little stars, honored him with a hero's funeral as a general in the KGB, and proclaimed him to be a great warrior in the people's cause. It's amazing how much death does for some folks.

15

JOHN CAIRNCROSS

THE ONE THAT GOT AWAY

JOHN CAIRNCROSS IS KNOWN AS "THE FIFTH MAN," AS HE WAS THE fifth of the Cambridge Five to be publicly identified. He was the actual working class man of the Cambridge Five—the only one from the class of people that Soviet communism claimed to be all about. Unaware that his despised Cambridge classmates were fellow spies, Cairncross fed information to the Soviets on everything from Nazi movements during WWII to German SS personnel files to the details of how NATO would be organized and funded. Unlike three of those despised Cambridge Five classmates, Cairncross never did experience the joys of the Soviet "workers' paradise." Instead, he became a revered professor at universities in the United States.

Remind us sometime to tell you about the heavy investments the Soviets made to permanently influence our US educational system. But for now . . .

The future Soviet spy John Cairncross was born the last of eight children in Lesmahagow, Scotland, on July 25, 1913. Unlike the other four members of the Cambridge Five, John came from a lower working class family. His father was an ironmonger and his

mother was a schoolteacher. Whatever Cairncross may have
lacked in aristocratic connections, he more than made up for in
intellect. At every step of his impressive education, he was recognized for his brilliance, which apparently ran in the family. All
three of his older brothers became highly successful university
professors and were recognized as leaders in their respective
fields.

Cairncross started his education by qualifying for an academic
scholarship to Hamilton Academy in Scotland. Hamilton was
rated as Scotland's best preparatory academy, and the competi-
tion for entry was rigorous. Cairncross progressed from Hamilton
to Glasgow University, where he received a degree in foreign
language. He then attended La Sorbonne in Paris and received
another degree in romance languages. After graduating from La
Sorbonne, he returned to England and studied at Cambridge in
1934. In 1936, he graduated from Cambridge with degrees in
German and French.

While at Cambridge, Cairncross met Anthony Blunt, Kim Philby,
and Guy Burgess. They shared left wing philosophies and sympathies for the Soviet Union, but had little else in common. Blunt
and Philby claimed that they saw Cairncross as an anti-social,
intellectual snob. As for Cairncross, he took a disliking to all
three of his future fellow spies. He apparently felt that they were
intellectually overrated, and that they thought far too much of
themselves and their high births.

After graduating from Cambridge, Cairncross sat for the British
Civil Service exam and placed first on the list for both the British
Foreign Office and the British Home Office. He was posted to the
British Foreign Office.

Based on an overall review of the reports and documents on
Cairncross, Holmes believes Cairncross agreed to work for the
Soviets before he ever sat for the exam. Blunt knew that Cairn-

cross was a communist sympathizer, and Blunt would have reported that to his handler—likely Alexander Orlov at that moment in time. This would have gotten to the NKVD's UK head of recruiting, Arnold Deutsch, an idealistic Czech/Austrian with no diplomatic cover who was working in the British Foreign Office.

James Klugmann, an active member of the Communist Party in the UK who was already in the NKVD fold, was sent by Deutsch or by someone else in the NKVD to recruit Cairncross. Klugmann's plan of attack for recruitment relied on his and Cairncross's shared admiration for Marxism and Cairncross's antipathy for the British establishment. Cairncross was a man of passionate opinions and feelings, and it is likely he had made up his mind to work for the communist cause in some capacity before he was ever approached by the Soviets. He proved to be an easy recruit.

Holmes has read several claims that Cairncross joined the Communist Party in 1937, but these claims are still debated today. It may have been Cairncross's lack of known affiliations to any communist groups that made him so useful to the Soviets. Holmes suspects that Cairncross tried to join the Communist Party in 1937, and the Soviets instead recruited him as an agent. However, these details are still hotly debated in the United Kingdom, and people in the UK intelligence community and their historians are not all in agreement on the topic.

Cairncross was hired to work in the Cabinet Office as a private secretary to Lord Hankey, the Chancellor of the Duchy of Lancaster. The preponderance of the evidence indicates that while working for Hankey, Cairncross supplied the Soviets with Top Secret cabinet papers recording the political and military attitudes and decisions of the UK government.

Note we say "the preponderance of the evidence" rather than stating this as clear, undeniable fact. This is our best interpretation, and we are convinced, but others take different interpretations. We would remind you folks that history is a murky affair on the brightest of days. After all, "fake news" has been around since Ogg ran for cave mayor in 30,000 BC.

In 1942, Cairncross was assigned to British Government Code and Cypher School ("GCCS") which later became the Government Communications Head Quarters ("GCHQ"), where his brilliance and his language skills made him a natural choice for working on intercepted German communications. Cairncross was given access to the United Kingdom's most secret intercepts, known as the Ultra intercepts.

Ultra was the originally British program for interception and decryption of German and Italian signals. Thanks to a foresighted Polish patriot, a commercial copy of the German Enigma machine had been secreted out of Poland when the Nazis invaded Poland in 1939. The British were conducting a monumental effort at breaking Germany's Top Secret Enigma encoded information, and they were managing some stunning successes with Ultra.

It was during his tenure at GCCS that Cairncross did some of his most important work for the Soviets. By 1943, thanks to his more mundane and moderate lifestyle, the Soviets had decided that Cairncross was the most reliable and trustworthy of their Cambridge spies. The Soviets had the highest confidence in whatever he sent them.

In the spring of 1943, Germany faced tough choices concerning their Eastern Front, and they needed to reformulate their war plans. During the previous winter, thanks to the combined idiocy of Adolf Hitler and Luftwaffe Commander Hermann Göring, the German 6th Army had been ordered to remain in place rather than retreat to a defensible position in the Ukraine.

Goering had assured Hitler that the 6th Army could easily be supplied by air. Only egomaniacal jackasses like Göring and his ardent Nazi sidekick, Hans Jeschonneck, could have arrived at such a conclusion. Only a delusional psychopath like Hitler could have believed such nonsensical advice against the pleading of his brilliant Wehrmacht general staff. The result of this combined idiocy was the destruction of a starved out German 6th Army.

At Stalingrad, the Germans, Romanians, and Italians lost about 800,000 troops, including 90,000 captured Germans. Of the 90,000 captured Germans, only 5,000 survived captivity in the Soviet Union and returned to Germany after the war. On the other side, the Soviets suffered 1,130,000 casualties at Stalingrad, including 14,000 Soviet soldiers who were executed for infractions real or imagined.

The Germans troops were better trained and had better equipment, but the Soviets had far more troops and equipment and could more easily absorb the losses. With British and American forces growing by the day in England, the Germans could not afford to wage a war of attrition with the Soviets. The Germans had to return to their blitzkrieg armored tactics that were so successful prior to Stalingrad, or they had to withdraw to defensible prepared positions closer to Germany and seek an armistice with the Soviet Union. Hitler insisted on a new offensive.

The German army prepared for a massive assault on the Soviet Kursk pocket codenamed Operation Citadel. The operation was planned in minute detail, and the plan was backed up with new Tiger tanks and later-generation Panther tanks. The plan made complete sense. The massive, mechanized forces and the new heavily-armored German tanks were in position to encircle the Soviet armies inside the huge Kursk salient. But there was one problem in the German plan. Thanks to John Cairncross, the Soviets knew every last detail of it.

The British had uncovered details of the German plans from a number of sources, including Ultra intercepts. They had no desire to trust the Soviets with information about the sources of their intelligence, but they were willing to share the resultant intelligence product, and they did so. Both the United States and the United Kingdom informed Stalin of the coming German attack. Unfortunately, Stalin operated on the false premise that the West would think and behave like he thought and behaved. Stalin believed that any information shared freely by his "allies" would be false, and that only information gained through espionage could be trusted.

Fortunately for the Soviet Union, John Cairncross gave Stalin what he wanted—the Ultra intercepts concerning Germany's pending attack on Kursk. Due to those intercepts, the Soviets were able to prepare multiple defensive layers in the best positions. They built well-camouflaged, reinforced anti-tank gun positions, tank traps, and mine fields in the exact path of the German attacks, concentrating 1,100,000 anti-tank mines in just the right locations. Artillery was pre-sighted on the right locations and ready to fire. Using alloys provided by the United States, the Soviets were able to design and manufacture higher-velocity, hardened anti-tank ammunition that could penetrate the new German tank hulls. The Germans attacked on July 4, 1943, and the results of the battle were disastrous for the German military.

Operation Citadel marked the end of meaningful offensive action by the German Army on the Eastern Front. After Operation Citadel, the Allies were able to almost completely take and maintain the initiative against Germany. Except for Hitler's last-ditch winter offensive against the West in December of 1944, the Allies were able to choose the time, place, and nature of major engage-ments against the German army. Even if it *was* the same favor that the Allies were attempting to openly do for Stalin, John Cairncross had done a great favor for his Soviet masters.

Some also credit Cairncross with giving the Soviet Union the first notice that the United States was pursuing the production of an atomic bomb. It is possible that Cairncross delivered an early report to the Soviet Union indicating that British scientists had concluded that making an atom bomb was feasible. However, the United States began its atomic project in in 1939, and the United Kingdom and the United States did not decide to cooperate on atomic bomb development until early 1942. When we overlay that timeline with a timeline of Cairncross's career postings, it seems likely that the Soviet Union received information on the project before Cairncross's reports.

In 1944, Cairncross was transferred to Section 5 of MI-6. At MI-6, Cairncross worked under his old Cambridge acquaintance and fellow Soviet spy, Kim Philby. Cairncross maintained that he did not, at that time, know that Philby was a fellow Soviet spy. Given the knowledge shared by Philby, Burgess, Maclean, and Anthony Blunt, this might seem unlikely. Nonetheless, Holmes finds it plausible. Cairncross shared anti-establishment sentiments and communist sympathies with the rest of the Cambridge Five, but he was not part of their social group. He did not sleep with any of them or drink with them. He considered them to be beneath him intellectually and identified them as part of the establishment that he hated. At the same time, the rest of the Cambridge Five considered Cairncross to be anti-social and completely lacking in any sense of humor. Also, in the case of Cairncross, the Soviets had no reason to violate the principal of compartmentalization by cluing him in. It was likely long after the Cambridge days that Cairncross became aware of the other members of the Cambridge Five.

By 1944, the Allies were beginning to look beyond the war and were concerned with what obstacles they might face in rebuilding post-war Europe. By then, it was clear that the Soviet Union would not be a cooperative partner in that effort.

As his MI-6 superior, Philby tasked Cairncross with building an Order of Battle for the Nazi SS forces. This, in essence, was to provide the United Kingdom with a sort of "map" for understanding Nazi allegiances within Germany. By capturing, killing, and possibly turning key SS members, the Allies hoped to weaken any die-hard resistance at the end of the war. It was also to identify possible intelligence sources for the closing days of the war and for the post-war era.

Cairncross was given access to all files on SS members, and he passed them on to the Soviets. The Soviets were able to use the information to build the East German intelligence services after WWII. The United States and the United Kingdom did something similar after the war, although the Soviet Union and the future NATO allies had different concepts about what post-war European intelligence services would be doing.

After WWII ended, Cairncross took a job for Her Majesty's Treasury. It seems likely that he did so at the suggestion of Yuri Modin, the Soviet handler of the Cambridge Five from 1944-1955. During his time at the Treasury, Cairncross provided the Soviets with another intelligence windfall. He gave them complete details of how NATO would be organized and funded.

After the Soviet Union dissolved, Cambridge Five handler Yuri Modin claimed that Cairncross had provided the Soviets with details of NATO's intentions to house US atomic weapons in NATO countries. This assertion by Modin strikes Holmes as unlikely simply because NATO did not make decisions about US nuclear weapons being based in Western Europe until after Cairncross left the Treasury in 1951.

In the spring of 1951, Guy Burgess and Donald Maclean escaped to the Soviet Union just as MI-5 investigators were about to bring Maclean in for interrogation. During a subsequent search of Burgess's home, a cache of stolen documents was found. At least one of these documents was attached to a hand written note from John Cairncross.

When Cairncross was questioned, he was well-prepared. Modin had assumed that Cairncross might be implicated, and he tutored Cairncross about what to admit and what to deny. Cairncross admitted to communist sympathies but denied ever spying. He claimed that he had been friends with Burgess, but that he had no knowledge of any illegal activities by Burgess. Cairncross didn't slip up in interrogation, and MI-5 was unable to establish enough evidence for a prosecution. He was forced to admit to carelessness with government documents, but espionage could not be proved. Burgess was, after-all, a fellow civil servant with a secret clearance when Cairncross gave him the documents in question.

Cairncross was forced to resign. The Soviet Union provided him with cash and perhaps connections to gain employment at Northwestern University in Evanston, Illinois and at Case Western Reserve University in Cleveland, Ohio. Cairncross quickly developed a reputation in romance languages and published several well-received academic works.

He must have been convinced that his past life as a Soviet spy was safely behind him. However, after Kim Philby defected to Moscow in 1963, MI-5 investigator Arthur Martin showed up at Cairncross's doorstep in Cleveland. Martin bluffed a confession from Cairncross, and Cairncross traded his fellow Soviet spy, Anthony Blunt, for his freedom. Cairncross always claimed he quit working for the Russians after WWII, but that was a lie. Unfortunately, his confession to Martin was not eligible to be used in British courts because it was made outside of UK jurisdiction. Cairncross did not go to prison for his treason.

After making his confessions, Cairncross moved to Italy and was employed by the United Nations in their world food program. Cairncross also worked for two major banks while in Italy. However, when he showed a sharp interest in one of the bank's private research on economic impacts of a possible Middle Eastern war, one of his coworkers became suspicious. Those suspicions were not reported to the Italian government at the time. Interestingly, though, Cairncross spent a year in prison for currency trading violations during his stay in Italy. Then, when a journalist tracked down Cairncross in Italy in December of 1979 and publicly identified him as "The Fifth Man" of the Cambridge Five, Cairncross moved to France.

In 1989, Soviet defector Colonel Oleg Gordievsky* gave evidence to MI-5 concerning Cairncross's activities as a spy. Gordievsky had been assigned to work on the writing of a KGB history for internal use by the KGB, and he had access to a broad range of files. Eventually, Gordievsky obtained a file that included Cairncross's identity, along with his code name. Gordievsky had worked as a double agent for the United Kingdom since the Soviet invasion of Czechoslovakia in 1968, and his information has consistently proven to be accurate over time.

During the last years of his life, Cairncross worked on a biography. While it is a better read than Philby's nonsensical tale, it is laced with falsehoods. Cairncross claimed that he stopped passing information to the Soviets after the war ended. We know this to be false. He also claimed that he never actually spied because, after-all, the Soviet Union was an ally.

After the fall of the Soviet Union, many Russians felt that the best way to keep Russia safe from the KGB was to open their archives so that the Russian public could see precisely how badly the KGB had acted against the Russian people. Before Czar Putin re-closed the KGB archives, the United States and the United Kingdom were both able to retrieve copies of nearly six thousand documents that Cairncross had sent to the Soviet Union.

The Soviet documents did not explain Cairncross's possible spying while he was in Italy. It may be that Cairncross was spying for cash for any number of governments or organizations without Soviet knowledge. It may be that the Soviets were still involved with him while he was in Italy, and that the files were not made available. However, the fact that Cairncross retired to France after being released from an Italian prison begs the question of whether he might have been spying for the French government or for French bankers while in Italy.

In 1995, Cairncross returned to England and married American opera star Gayle Brinkerhoff. A few months later, he suffered a series of strokes and died in Hertfordshire, England on October 8.

Yuri Modin was often exasperated by Cairncross's lack of punctuality in meetings, as well as his refusal to photograph documents rather than remove them from UK government offices for copying. Modin also couldn't understand how Cairncross could repeatedly get away with his open disdain for members of the British ruling class that held so much power in British bureaucracies. Nevertheless, Modin claimed that Cairncross had been his favorite of the Cambridge traitors to work with and the most valuable of the group. Certainly Cairncross, who wrote thank you notes to the Soviet Union whenever they paid him for information, was the most pleasant. It may well be that he most matched Modin's ideal of a fellow communist. Compared to dealing with the hard-drinking and flamboyant Burgess, the philandering Philby, the egotistical Blunt, and the depressed and bitter Maclean, working with the sober, highly-productive Cairncross might have been a joy, but for the United Kingdom and the West, Cairncross was a deadly plague that was not eradicated soon enough.

* **C**olonel Oleg Gordievsky, a KGB officer, became a double agent working for the United Kingdom after the brutal Soviet invasion of Czechoslovakia in August of 1968. He defected to the West in 1985.

16

CHRISTOPHER BOYCE AND ANDREW DAULTON LEE

THE FALCON AND THE SNOWMAN

WHEN WE STUDY THE CASES OF TRAITORS, THERE IS ALWAYS AN overarching question . . . How did they get that far? With the Cambridge Five, elitism blinded the spy hunters of MI-5 and MI-6 to the treachery in their own upperclass ranks. In the case of The Falcon and The Snowman, a sociopath and a drug dealer who never should have gotten anywhere near classified information, the blinders were secured by nepotism.

In Santa Monica, California, in 1953, a recently retired FBI agent named Charles Boyce and his wife Noreen were blessed with the birth of their first child. They named their future altar boy Christopher. Noreen Boyce was a strict Catholic who avoided birth control, and eventually she gave Christopher eight younger siblings. Charles Boyce had a successful career as a security expert in the aerospace industry, and even with nine children, the family enjoyed a life of affluence with a home in the fashionable Palos Verdes community. Charles and Noreen Boyce were politically conservative and outspokenly patriotic. FBI agents and other law enforcement friends frequently visited their home.

Undoubtedly, the successful parents had no idea that their oldest would one day betray their country.

Christopher Boyce attended a Catholic elementary school, where he flourished both academically and socially. He embraced Catholicism and was an enthusiastic altar boy at the local church. He made friends easily, and his best friend was a fellow altar boy by the name of Andrew Daulton Lee. Unlike the popular "A" student Boyce, Lee struggled to maintain a "C" average and was socially awkward, but they shared something important—they were both known to be a daredevils, even in their elementary school days.

On one occasion, Boyce's love of risk-taking led to a fall from a forty-foot tree. He landed in a pile of leaves on a muddy river bed and survived. Though he suffered two compressed disks in his back, the injury did not dampen his love of thrill seeking. Then, as teenagers, Boyce and Lee took up the hobby of falconry. Boyce became fairly expert at it, hence his eventual name, "The Falcon."

During high school, the two lost their enthusiasm for the Catholic Church and decided that they were no longer Christian. Boyce's grades slipped, but he remained popular with his fellow students. Lee's grades remained poor, and he replaced his love of church with a love of cocaine. Though he'd previously had trouble attracting female companionship, he was able to use marijuana and cocaine to obtain sex with cooperative girls. He thus obtained the nickname, "The Snowman."

If we are to understand the eventual criminal misadventures of Boyce and Lee, a.k.a. The Falcon and The Snowman, we should consider the time in which they were raised. By the late 60s, the Vietnam War was on the news every night, and the major media networks generally took a dim view of the federal government's atrocious mismanagement of that conflict. The great American

Optimism of the 40s and 50s had been replaced with cynicism and a healthy mistrust of authority.

After Boyce and Lee graduated high school, Boyce started college, and Lee expanded his drug business. Lee did hold legitimate jobs on occasion, but the low wages and long hours held no appeal when the easy money of drug dealing was available. Besides, as The Snowman, a successful cocaine dealer, he held a certain place of importance in the social circles of affluent youths who had never accepted him prior to his drug dealing career.

Christopher Boyce floundered in college and dropped out. At his parents' urging and support, he started college again and dropped out again, and again. Boyce was certainly smart enough for school, but he had no interest. His parents were worried about their bright son's seemingly dull future. His father had a close friend who was the security director at TRW Corporation, so Christopher's father asked that friend if he could help find a job for Christopher. TRW hired Chris Boyce as a clerk in 1974.

TRW manufactured components for highly-advanced Top Secret communications and reconnaissance satellites for the CIA and other federal agencies. Christopher Boyce worked at a TRW facility that was equipped to receive and decode information from US satellites. Thanks to his dad's influence, Boyce, with no post-high school education, no legitimate experience, and no security screening, was given a security badge and access to classified documents at TRW.

To the average reader, this might seem outrageously careless of TRW. It was. And if that wasn't bad enough, Boyce was soon given Top Secret clearances by the CIA and the NSA.

If a proper investigation had been done, and if anyone had bothered to analyze the results, Boyce's lack of any track record and three successive drop outs from three different colleges would have indicated a glaring lack of maturity and reliability. However, Boyce did not even receive a lie-detector test, which, while not foolproof, would likely have uncovered his drug history and the fact that his best friend was the local "Snowman." Apparently, the simple lack of an arrest record and his father's reputation were enough to propel Chris Boyce from an entry-level status to Top Secret access within a few months of his joining TRW.

Boyce was transferred to an even higher position in the "Black Vault" at TRW. This was where the company stored Top Secret codes, and where incoming data from satellites were decoded. We now know that Boyce discovered a party atmosphere within the Black Vault team. Safe in the knowledge that visitors were not allowed in the vault, the Black Vault team was using a CIA shredding machine as a daiquiri mixer. It literally was a party.

After being promoted to the Black Vault team, Boyce began reading decoded messages that were apparently being misrouted to TRW. These included diplomatic messages. Boyce claims that, in combination with his anger at the Vietnam War, the content of some of the messages caused him to decide to turn against the United States.

One series of messages that Boyce pointed to was supposed diplomatic traffic indicating that the United States was plotting the downfall of the Australian Prime Minister Gough Whitlam. According to Boyce, the US government was angry at Australia because it was "threatening to pull out of Vietnam." The United States was, indeed, unhappy with Gough and his anti-American views, but Boyce's story sounds like something that was fed to him in contingency planning by a Soviet KGB handler. Australia pulled its last combat forces out of Vietnam in 1972, two years prior to Boyce's joining TRW and beginning his career as a spy for the Soviet Union. The United States pulled out its last combat troops in Vietnam in 1973. The "Australia" line in Boyce's justifications of his betrayal makes no sense.Christopher Boyce's motivations for betraying the United States were likely far less noble than he claims.

Boyce copied and stole documents and codes from the Black Vault to sell them to the Soviet Union. In a lapse of judgment, he decided to use Andrew Daulton Lee as his go-between to communicate with the Soviets. While drug dealers and all variety of criminals are often used in intelligence operations, they are not usually trusted with more than the minimal information they need for a particular task. They are never trusted to act as couriers. Boyce had read a couple of spy novels, but apparently not the right ones. Given Lee's basic emotional insecurity and his drug use, he was a bad choice, but Lee was the one person who Boyce could trust in terms of personal loyalty.

The Snowman was thrilled with Boyce's suggestion that they spy for the Soviet Union, and he quickly agreed. In Lee's mind, the chance to help Boyce spy on the US government seemed like the perfect opportunity. By that time, Lee had already served prison time for dealing cocaine and heroin, and, after being busted on drug charges again, he had worked as a snitch for the police. Lee knew enough about the drug dealing world to know that his long-term prospects for health and happiness as a snitch were rather dim. For him, spying not only meant money, but the chance to broaden his criminal horizons. It also provided the emotionally fragile Lee with a sense of importance. Lee purchased spy novels for his training regimen and travelled to Mexico City to contact the Soviet Embassy. Thus began the espionage careers of The Falcon and The Snowman.

Once in Mexico City, Lee made a personal visit to the Soviet Embassy, where he told the receptionist that he had most important information for the Soviets. The receptionist alerted senior resident KGB officer Vasiliy Okana, and Okana agreed to interview Lee in a secure room in the embassy. Intelligence veteran Okana was well-educated, well-trained, and experienced. He was used to using patience and hard work to gather intelligence. Based on his long experience, Lee seemed like one more crackpot, third-rate crook trying to run a second-rate spy scam.

Unfortunately for the United States, Okana listened to Lee dispassionately in spite of the horrible first impression that Lee made on him. By the end of the conversation, Okana realized that, although Lee was indeed a flake, he likely was working for someone with access to valuable information. Okana decided to invest time, effort, and scarce KGB cash to see what information Lee could supply.

Working with Lee was an instant nightmare. The cocaine-snorting, booze-gulping amateur grew impatient and ignored the protocols and procedures that the KGB had given him to keep him safe from detection by the US and Mexican authorities. Even though Lee was told that the Soviet Embassy was under constant surveillance by the Mexican government and foreign intelligence services, Lee visited the embassy in person and demanded attention.

Lee knew that the KGB would have happily cut him out of the operation and replaced him with a professional KGB courier, so Lee was careful to not identify Boyce to the Soviets. Okana and his boss must have had to exercise every last ounce of patience and persuasion to keep Lee from self-destructing. They despised Lee, but he served as a vital link between the KGB and the mysterious agent that was sending such a windfall of valuable intelligence.

In addition to daily message and telemetry codes, Boyce sent decoded messages and information about the satellites. We now know that the Soviets had other sources that were delivering the same technical intelligence about the same US spy satellite systems. However, the KGB was not about to tip its hand by failing to show an interest in the technical intelligence that Boyce was providing along with the precious codes and message copies.

In spite of having to rely on one of history's least talented spies as a go-between, the Soviets kept the operation working for two years. The damage that Christopher Boyce did to US security in that time was tremendous. The code strips allowed massive volumes of secret US communications around the world to be quickly decoded by the Soviet Union.

Besides having a clear picture of US military and diplomatic intentions, the information was a great help to the KGB's counter-intelligence efforts. His information was useful in corroborating intelligence the Soviets gleaned from other sources, and by adding valuable pieces to the many puzzles that the KGB was constantly trying to complete to identify spies in the Soviet system, Boyce indirectly helped the KGB round up people behind the Iron Curtain who were working for the West.

Somewhat predictably, on one of his chemically-enhanced, unwelcome visits to the Soviet Embassy in Mexico City, Lee aroused the suspicion of the Mexican police. They recognized him as a criminal, but they were mistaken about which particular flavor of criminal he was. The police arrested Lee on the belief that he had murdered a Mexican policeman.

Lee demanded his rights as a US citizen, and the Mexican police did what they always do to felony suspects—they laughed and then continued to torture him. Lee confessed to spying against the United States for the Soviets. The Mexicans realized that he was, in fact, not the criminal that they were looking for and deported him. When Lee crossed the border into the United States in January of 1977, he was arrested.

Using his full powers of intellect and every ounce of his self-discipline, Lee resisted the verbal interrogation at the hands of the FBI—for about two minutes. Then he talked a blue streak and identified his lifelong best friend, Christopher Boyce, as the source of the intelligence that he had been delivering to the Soviets. Had Lee been slightly brighter, he would have traded Boyce for a light sentence. He wasn't slightly brighter, so he spilled the beans in exchange for nothing.

The FBI and US Marshal Service quickly detained Boyce, capturing him on the seaside cliffs of Palo Verde. Boyce's last act before his arrest was to free his pet falcon.

The trial was remarkably speedy. It's possible the federal judges and prosecutors were in a hurry to get it done and out of the news. There was plenty of embarrassment to go around, and too many taxpayers might have asked too many questions about how much tax money they were giving TRW to allow so much Top Secret information stroll out their door.

By May of 1977, Christopher Boyce and Andrew Daulton Lee were convicted of spying for the Soviet Union. Boyce was given a 40-year sentence. Due to his higher number of convictions and the fact that he had violated his parole from prior drug dealing convictions, Lee was given a life sentence.

Boyce and Lee started serving their sentences in California at Federal Correctional Institute, Terminal Island. After a while, Boyce was moved to a jail in San Diego. We assume that the move was to make it easier for investigators to do follow-up interrogations, as authorities were never certain that they had the full story. Counterintelligence agents in the FBI and CIA likely wondered if there were even more spies at TRW.

On July 10, 1979, Boyce was transferred to a federal prison in Lompoc, California. Neither Boyce nor Lee was fond of prison life. The social status of a convicted traitor in prison is close to that of a pedophile, and life was appropriately unpleasant for them at the bottom of the prison social ladder.

But The Falcon's adventures were not quite over yet. . . .

Boyce was smart and patient enough to plan an escape. He took up jogging and ran laps to build his endurance. On January 21, 1980, Boyce escaped from Lompoc prison with the help of fellow inmates, a drainage hole to hide in, a makeshift ladder, and tin snips to cut the barbed-wire perimeter. He ran all night to gain as much distance as possible, stealing some clothes from a clothes line along the way to eluded capture. After Boyce's escape, Lee was moved to a higher security federal prison in Marion, Illinois. Lee claims that that ended his "friendship" with Boyce.

Now free but on the lam, Boyce faced serious challenges. How would he escape the notice of alert passersby or the occasional FBI agents and US Marshals that he might run into in the course of his days? How would he eat? Boyce's one career skill, the "my FBI daddy got me this job" option, was no longer available to him. So Boyce embarked on a new career in bank robbery as the cornerstone of his financial planning. He befriended a single mother with a strong anti-establishment, anti-social outlook, and she became his bank robbing accomplice.

Generally, bank robbers plan and execute robberies that are profitable enough to net the cash they need to keep them from having to take the risk too often. Bank robbery is a dangerous crime that can easily escalate to multiple murders. It also attracts the interest of major law enforcement assets such as the FBI and state police. Bank robberies in Western states have an additional risk in that sometimes an impatient customer doesn't like having their busy schedule interrupted by a snotty little bank robber, and they simply pull a weapon and shoot the crook. Unfortunately, Boyce never robbed a bank that we happened to be standing in, so we never got the chance to shoot him. Neither did anyone else.

Boyce and his pickup team of latter-day bank robbers may not have been too clear on the best model for successful heists, but they managed to rob seventeen banks without being killed or captured. We have to give them credit for getting away with their hides intact.

Boyce developed the alias of "Anthony Edward Lester." He knew he couldn't live as a fugitive in the United States forever, so he took flying lessons and planned to fly to the Soviet Union. He naively believed that the KGB would offer him an active commission as an officer in the Soviet military.

Ha. Haha. Hahahahaha.

The Soviet Union always maintained reputable training facilities for military officers. They turned out well-trained, intelligent officers, and Boyce would not have been given any sort of real commission. Might the Soviets have given him some cute medals and certificates to hang on the limited wall space of a small apartment in Moscow? Sure. Would they have given him a manuscript to sign off on and then published it for him? You bet they would have. Would the Soviets have been so dumb as to treat Boyce like a real adult and make him an active officer in the KGB or Soviet military? Unfortunately, they were always smarter than that. The Soviets would have probably propped him up for propaganda purposes, but his life in the Soviet Union would have been little better than life in a federal prison in the United States.

As Boyce gradually increased his piloting skills, the FBI and US Marshals Service were each conducting manhunts for him and closing in. In August of 1981, the feds received a viable tip from one of Boyce's bank robbery teammates that Boyce was in Port Angeles, Washington. A task force of eighteen US Marshals, six

FBI agents, and a US Border Patrol agent was formed and began a systematic investigation in Port Angeles.

Two US Marshals pulled in at a drive-in restaurant, The Pit Stop, on August 21, 1981, and cashed in all their serendipity chips for life. There at the drive-in sat Christopher Boyce. The temptation to immediately draw down on him must have been intense, but the Marshals were calm and disciplined. They called for backup. Once they had five agents in place, they arrested Boyce. Boyce received another conviction for his escape and was returned to prison.

Boyce and Lee were clearly guilty of espionage and deserved the infamy that came their way. In our view, they deserved worse than they got. That being said, Boyce never should have had access to the information that he sold to the Soviets in the first place.

The sloppy practices that allowed Boyce to steal Top Secret communications and telemetry codes so easily deserved close scrutiny by the federal government. If any such scrutiny occurred, it happened quietly and remains a well-guarded secret. Any ramifications for TRW Corporation, the NSA, the National Reconnaissance Office, and the CIA, if they occurred at all, were far better hidden than all of the Top Secret data in their collective care.

In recent years, both Boyce and Lee were paroled. Their life as spies is over, but questions remain about their cases. Why was there apparently no negative consequence to the people at TRW who were responsible for the handling and security of the Top Secret information? TRW has since been involved in other scandals, including hazardous workplace practices and the illegal dumping of dangerous chemicals. In spite of that, TRW and many other companies with histories of shabby security practices remain the beneficiaries of multibillion dollar defense and intelligence contracts.

Boyce and Lee were amateurs. Lee all but begged to be caught. But were there other, more sober employees at TRW and other contractors that remain at large? Since 9/11, we have seen sweeping changes in law enforcement and politics. The US Congress and the past and present Presidents all claim a desperate need for more invasive domestic surveillance in order that we might survive one more day, and yet we have the same open borders and the same sloppy handling of our own Top Secrets.

It is Holmes's considered opinion that what occurred at TRW in the 70s could still be happening there today. It could also be happening at any other contractor that handles secret information for the US government. That being said, Private Bradley Manning, Lt. Cmdr. Edward Lin (See *Spycraft: Critical Moments in Espionage*), the dirtbags of the Fat Leonard Conspiracy, and others have demonstrated that it can just as easily still be happening with US government employees, as well.

Remember the old saying about closing the barn door after the horse has escaped? The Falcon has long since fallen, and The Snowman melted, but in our ever-increasing zeal to know everything about every citizen, have we even bothered to close the barn door? We hope we are wrong, but we don't think so.

17

BRADLEY/BREANNA/CHELSEA MANNING
THE SOLDIER THAT NEVER SHOULD HAVE BEEN ONE

THE CAMBRIDGE FIVE GOT AWAY WITH THEIR TREASONS BECAUSE they hid behind their upper-class privilege. The Falcon and The Snowman took advantage of the privilege afforded by nepotism. Then we come to Bradley/Breanna/Chelsea Manning, who, like Christopher Boyce, should never have gotten near classified information in the first place. Some would put off her unqualified and continued access to classified materials to sloppy recruiting, some would say it was due to a lax US Army discipline system, and some would put it off to the "privilege" enjoyed by those at the forefront of popular political trends. We would say all are correct. She never should have been recruited in the first place, and once she was, she never should have gotten past toilet cleaning detail.

Bradley/Breanna/Chelsea Manning is one of the most controversial figures in modern American espionage history. To some, she is a hero of transgender identity politics. To some, she is a "whistleblower" who revealed the US Army's dirty laundry. To some, she is a "leaker" who leaked information to WikiLeaks to be published on the internet. To most, however, she is a low-life, woman-beating traitor who deliberately betrayed her own fellow military troops and our Afghani allies, with a death and destruction tally that is still being counted.

Though Manning has had many names, she likes to be called Chelsea now. While we could not care less if traitors are "she," "he," "it," "they," or any other pronoun, for the purposes of this chapter, we will call Manning "Bradley" and "him" for the time she was a man named Bradley, "Breanna" and "she" for the time when she was Breanna, and "Chelsea" and "she" for the time after she decided to change her name again. We can't be responsible for anything either she or we might call her after the publication of this book.

On December 17, 2011, news channels in the United States and Europe reported on US Army Private Bradley Manning's pretrial hearing in Fort Meade, Maryland. Manning was responding to charges that he passed over 250,000 classified US diplomatic messages, nearly 500,000 secret military files, over 400,000 medical files of military personnel, and the names of Afghan double agents cooperating with the US military to unauthorized parties.

We're going to pause a moment to allow you to take in those numbers. . . .

As for the betrayal of over 400,000 fellow military personnel whose medical files Bradley passed on, it is worth noting that the computer industry considers medical information to be the most valuable information on the internet. That's because it never changes, and it can be used by both criminal entities and foreign governments for identity theft, blackmail, stalking, subversion, and any number of other nefarious purposes. Four hundred thousand of our military service men and women were compromised.

Worse still, the US military reported that after Bradley supplied WikiLeaks with the names of those Afghan double agents who put their lives and the lives of their families in our hands to work with us, and WikiLeaks published those names, most of them were killed by the Taliban or Tali-clones. We aren't at liberty to share any of the specifics about those people who were murdered, but they were sons, daughters, brothers, sisters, mothers, and fathers—real people with real histories and real loved ones who trusted the US military and intelligence communities in their efforts to make their corner of the world a better place for themselves and for their families. Now they are dead because of Bradley Manning, and anyone else who would have worked with the United States is rightfully thinking twice.

We're going to pause a moment to let that sink in, as well. . . .

So precisely who is Bradley/Breanna/Chelsea Manning, and why isn't she dangling at the end of a rope?

Bradley Manning was born on December 17, 1987 in Crescent, Oklahoma to the Welsh woman Susan Fox and her American husband Brian Manning. According to his teachers, Bradley was outspoken about his opinions, but he was not a troublemaker.

When Bradley was thirteen, his parents divorced and he moved to Wales with his mother. In school in Wales, Manning was bullied. This was possibly exacerbated by his outspokenness, his effeminate mannerisms, and his likely lack of social skills. He eventually took an academic equivalency test and moved back to Oklahoma to live with his father.

In the United States, Manning landed a job with a software company but was fired after a few months. Then, in March of 2006, he got into an argument with his stepmother and decided to make his point by threatening her with a butcher knife. The police removed Manning from the house. After that, he lived in an old pickup truck and worked at odd jobs.

In October of 2007, Bradley entered the Army. He scored well on various tests and was selected for training in Army Intelligence School. While in intelligence school at Fort Huachuca in Arizona, Manning was reprimanded for posting sensitive information on YouTube. Even at that early stage in his military career, he was deliberately violating security protocols.

At that point, had Holmes been his commanding officer, Manning would have begun his brilliant new Army career as a Bathroom Cleaning and Parking Lot Security Specialist. Holmes simply would have explained to Bradley that if any vehicles in the parking lot went damaged, he would be pulling extra duty on weekends cleaning everyone else's toilets. It's a big Army with lots of toilets, and they need lots of cleaning, so there is a place for the Bradley Mannings of the military world, but that place should never have included access to weapons, classified information, vehicles, computers, electricity, etc.

However, in the Western world, the modern military doesn't always like the hardass approach, so Bradley was graduated, and he and his security clearance, which must have been conducted by a Taliban subcontractor, were designated to eventually work in Iraq. Iraq at the time was a place with an abundance of secret American military communications, weapons, vehicles, things that go "boom," and occasionally even electricity—not at all the sort of place for Bradley Manning.

Before being deployed to Iraq, Manning spent time at Fort Drum, New York, the home of the elite 10th Mountain Division. While at Fort Drum, he hooked up with a male lover from Boston College who introduced him to the hacker community. Bradley attended a "hackerspace" workshop where he presumably honed his hackiness. Manning was unhappy at Fort Drum and didn't hide it. He argued with his roommates and screamed at officers. Still, nobody saw any reason to pull his security clearance.

To a degree, we can understand this. In the US military, intelligence personnel of all varieties are expected to be a bit eccentric. Some of them often ignore petty rules and find ways to get around the system without ruffling any high-ranking feathers. If they do good work, the commanders will usually look the other way rather than troubling to find new talent to complete difficult tasks that not everyone is capable of doing.

In exchange for this informal different-drummer exception that intelligence personnel might at times receive, they are expected to maintain the highest security standards and perform their corps responsibilities at outstanding levels. However, that willingness to ignore a few eccentricities does not usually extend to screaming at superior officers or fighting with roommates. Manning was marching to his own drummer, but he clearly was not maintaining good security practices. He was sent to a mental health counselor, but his security clearance was not revoked.

In October of 2009, Manning was sent to Iraq and stationed at Forward Operating Base Hammer. While at FOB Hammer, Manning's state of mind did not improve. Several people reported his odd behavior, and he was sent to a chaplain.

If a chaplain is in residence at a forward operating base, he will often serve as minister, psychiatrist, counselor, and social worker all rolled into one. Unfortunately, even a talented chaplain has limited tools at his disposal and can't remove a disturbed patient from the front. Not surprisingly, the chaplain was unable to perform any magic on Manning, and Manning's behavior did not improve.

Manning had access to a vast array of data—data that his job did not require—via the Secret Internet Protocol Router Network and the Joint Worldwide Intelligence Communications System. Apparently, he was only in theater about a month when he started sending WikiLeaks volumes of classified files.

Then, on May 7, 2010, Manning punched his female commanding officer in the face. Fortunately for Manning, she did not draw her M9 pistol and shoot him twice. Manning was demoted to the rank of private and told that he would be sent home and discharged. Nevertheless, he kept his access to classified information.

Shortly after the woman-beating incident and before he was shipped home, Bradley reached out to famous ex-hacker Adrian Lamo. Manning and Lamo chatted online, and Manning bragged to Lamo about the files that he had sent to Julian Assange at WikiLeaks. Lamo realized that the lives of US servicemen and their allies were at stake, and he contacted the FBI. Lamo gave the FBI the classified files that Manning had sent him, along with logs of their chats.

Manning was arrested on May 26, 2010, by the US Army and placed in custody in Kuwait. He was charged on July 5, 2010 with transferring classified information to unauthorized parties while knowing that it would be used to harm the United States of America.

On July 29, 2010, Manning was transferred to the Marine Corps brig in Quantico, Virginia. Manning and his supporters claimed that he was held in inhumane conditions in Quantico, but even his own lawyer, David Coombs, said he was not tortured or mistreated. Then, on April 11, 2011, Manning was transferred to a medium security facility at Fort Leavenworth, Kansas, where he was held under less stringent conditions.

In spite of the severe consequences of Manning's betrayal, Manning's defense team, with some success, marketed Manning as a heroic whistleblower, drawing supporters who created a "Free Bradley Manning Support Network." One middle-aged supporter interviewed by Reuters even said Manning should receive a Medal of Honor for his heroic acts.

Manning's defense team also introduced Manning's alter ego, "Breanna Manning," and claimed Breanna's actions were in part caused by the fact that, as a homosexual, she was treated unfairly by the military. Never mind the fact that thousands of homosexuals have served honorably in the US military, and though many certainly may have suffered unfair treatment and social rejection by their peers, almost none of them responded by leaking secret information. Nevertheless, a few of the more gullible gay rights advocates took up the clarion call and wanted Manning released from her Army homosexual persecution. The fact that the US Army had not charged Breanna with any Uniform Code of Military Justice violations based on her sexual practices did not stop those few souls from stridently defending Manning's gay rights.

In August of 2013, Manning announced that she prefers to be addressed as "Chelsea Manning" rather than "Breanna Manning." That same month, the military justice system determined that Manning was guilty and sentenced her to thirty-five years in prison. Given the rules of the system, Manning would have been eligible for a parole hearing in 2023—in all a sentence we and many others considered lenient for someone who punched her commanding officer in the face and transferred hundreds of thousands of classified documents to WikiLeaks, violating the medical privacy rights of her fellow military personnel, complicating the work our US diplomats do, and, most importantly, enabling the murder of our agents.

However, Chelsea Manning's defense team had managed to persuade a significant percentage of the public and the vast majority of the media to view her as a heroic whistleblower. The

defense and the media promoted Manning as being likable, artic-
ulate, and reasonable—a newer, shinier, more sincere version of
herself—and pushed the line that Manning was no different from
NSA whistleblower Edward Snowden.

The fact is that, while a few of the files that Manning sent to
WikiLeaks may have been classified in order to protect the US
Army from embarrassing mistakes that resulted in civilian deaths
in Iraq and Afghanistan, the vast majority of what Manning gave
away, such as the medical files and the names of our agents, could
hardly qualify as suitable material for whistleblowing. Further-
more, if whistleblowing had been Manning's goal, military
personnel have access to whistleblowing channels that they can
use without fear of prosecution or retaliation. The idea that any
whistleblowing could legitimately include such a release is
preposterous.

In another vein, Chelsea Manning wanted a sex change operation. At the same time that her defenders were attributing her
persecution as a homosexual for her treasonous behavior,
Chelsea was saying she was not gay, that she was actually a
woman, and that the stress from gender identity issues was the
reason for the treason.

Regardless of any angst Manning may have experienced, given
the volume of information she gave away, it will take decades to
completely assess the damage done, but it is not too soon for us
to be certain that Manning did not act out of concern for her
fellow humans. It seems more likely that she wanted to take
revenge on an Army that she felt had rejected her. She succeeded.

Another sad consequence of the highly-successful Bradley/Bre-
anna/Chelsea image makeover is that too little attention was paid
to the fact that such an obviously bad soldier was able to keep
such high access to classified information for so long. In an organization the size of the US Army, there will always be individuals

suffering from a variety of emotional problems and psychiatric conditions. The Army needs to do a better job of keeping them away from weapon systems and classified information.

In spite of the fact that Manning's release of the names of our Afghan agents subsequently got most of them killed, Manning's defense team loudly and absurdly proclaimed "no one was harmed by Private Manning's actions." They and the media pushed the line that Manning acted out of patriotic concern for the welfare of the United States.

The court of public opinion—that mob that is always short on facts and legal knowledge and long on opinion—was seduced by Manning's plea. In spite of Manning's calculated traitorous breaches, Manning became a leftist *cause célèbre*. Her celebrity was increased by the fact that she is transgender at a time when transgender issues have come of age. Manning's fan club called for a full pardon.

President Obama heard the call. Obama did not pardon Manning, but he did commute all but four months of her sentence on January 17, 2017. Obama chose to characterize Manning as a "leaker" rather than a traitor, in spite of the aid Manning's actions gave to our enemies and the deaths she caused. Obama stated that Manning's sentence of thirty-five years was out of proportion to the crime of "leaking." Chelsea Manning was released from prison after serving only seven years.

Once out, Manning continued to pursue an appeal in the US Army Court of Criminal Appeals that would have cleared her name. Her defense argued that Manning had a First Amendment Freedom of Speech right to leak the classified information to the press, claiming the Espionage Act is vague in its definition of what actually relates to national defense. Because, you know, some classified markings are really just suggestions, right? . . . Yeah. The judges didn't buy it, either. The US Army Court of

Criminal Appeals fully upheld Manning's conviction and sentencing. Manning's attorneys will now take the appeal to the Court of Appeals for the Armed Forces.

And here's the kicker. As long as Manning is appealing her conviction through the military courts, she is *still on active duty*. That means that even though she is on "excess leave" and not being paid a salary, she is still receiving the full healthcare and benefits of a loyal active duty American soldier. That's because the Uniform Code of Military Justice only applies to those who are in the military or who are civilians serving alongside military personnel in the field during a declared war or a contingency operation.

Manning, perhaps emboldened by her fan club, decided to run for the US Senate in the State of Maryland in 2018. She garnered 5.7% of the votes during the Democratic Primary in that state. One could look this outcome two ways. One could say, "She *only* got 5.7% of the vote." Or one could say, "Seriously? She conned 32,201 people into voting for a convicted traitor?"

Leaving politics to "prioritize [her] own well-being," Manning went on to make money with an international speaking tour, telling anyone who would listen that living in the United States is like living in prison. The tour ran into a hitch when the Government of Australia refused to grant Manning a visa for her speaking engagement. Manning took comfort in the welcoming arms of New Zealand.

In October 2018, Manning used that taxpayer-funded active duty healthcare benefit for her gender reassignment surgery. She then used her celebrity platform for transgender advocacy, continuing to cast herself as the true victim at every opportunity. She has never publicly expressed any remorse for her actions resulting in the deaths of our allies and the privacy violation of hundreds of thousands of military personnel.

And her story continues. As of the time of publication of this book, Manning has been popping in and out of prison for contempt of court because she refuses to testify in a case against WikiLeaks.

We still hope that the US Army, the US State Department, and the NSA are as upset as we are about Manning's ease of access to so much information, and we hope that the Army and all other branches of the military and government will consider showing a little more willingness to withhold security clearances and live ammo from individuals who are obviously mentally unstable. America has a newer, shinier Bradley/Breanna/Chelsea Manning to talk about. But do we have a more efficient and responsible government yet? That remains to be seen.

18

ROBERT HANSSEN

AT THE CORNER OF EGO AND TREASON

AGAIN WE FACE THE OVERWHELMINGLY OBVIOUS QUESTION WITH Robert Hanssen . . . How did he get away with this for so long? In short, Robert Hanssen is the American version of the Cambridge Five, in that his case is an American example of how institutional culture impacts operations.

Robert Philip Hanssen began his ignominious existence in Chicago, Illinois on April 18, 1944 and grew up in the Norwood Park area of the city. His father, Howard, was a police officer for the Chicago Police Department, and his mother, Vivien, was a housewife.

According to Hanssen and other witnesses, Howard emotionally abused Robert, constantly deriding him. Nothing Robert ever did was good enough. Howard thought Robert was a sissy, and he made sure Robert knew it. According to one report from Robert Hanssen's alma mater, Knox College, Howard Hanssen would come to the college to talk down Robert to his professors and to lobby against putting Robert on the Dean's List, saying it would go to his head. How much this abuse led to Robert Hanssen selling out his country for nothing more than ego gratification and a bit of filthy lucre is as much a matter of debate as it is irrelevant.

Robert was socially awkward as a youth. Like most kids, he was not particularly popular, but he also did not have an abundance of enemies, and his social life was unremarkable. He graduated from William Howard Taft High School in 1962 and went on to study chemistry at Knox College in Galesburg, Illinois. He also studied Russian and played intramural basketball. He was known for being a geek and a bookworm.

While in college, Hanssen spent his summers working at a mental institution, where he met co-worker Bernadette "Bonnie" Wauck, a sociology student at Loyola University. Hanssen wooed Bonnie with love letters throughout his senior year at Knox. They married in 1968 and proceeded to have six children. Bonnie was a devout conservative Roman Catholic, and during their courtship, Robert converted from his Lutheran roots to Catholicism. After converting, Robert became a particularly virtue-signaling Catholic. He joined Opus Dei, a conservative international Catholic organization, and he regularly annoyed other Catholics by criticizing them for not being Catholic enough.

Hanssen graduated from Knox with a Bachelor of Science in Chemistry in 1966. Though his field was chemistry, he was known to be highly computer-oriented from an early age, and that was where his interests lay. This crossover was not unusual at the time, as there were no dedicated computer science departments.

Hanssen tried to get a job as a cryptographer with the NSA but was unable to do so, possibly due to budget cuts. In lieu of a career with the NSA, Hanssen fulfilled his mother's dreams for him by enrolling in dental school at Northwestern University. However, dental school was not to his liking. He dropped from the program and instead got an MBA in accounting in 1971. Then, in 1972, Hanssen obtained a job doing forensic accounting with the Internal Affairs branch of the Chicago Police Department. Three years later, Robert went to work for the FBI. He had the perfect education and background to be useful to the Bureau. It also made him useful to the KGB.

Hanssen's first FBI assignment was Gary, Indiana. Later, in 1978, he was transferred to the field office in New York City, which was considered a plum assignment. It was his expertise in computers and information systems that landed him the position. That expertise also got his foot through the door into counterintelligence.

Hanssen was assigned the task of compiling a database concerning Soviet intelligence. As a result, nearly everything the FBI knew about Soviets and Soviet agents went through Robert's hands for the purpose of compiling the database. As early as 1979, Robert Hanssen took advantage of this access and approached the Soviet GRU about spying for them in exchange for money.

That's right. Money. The acronym MICE explains virtually every traitor. It stands for Money, Ideology, Compromise, and Ego. The idealistic Opus Dei devout Catholic sold out his countrymen for something as simple and straightforward as a little money and a great deal of vanity. The Soviets, of course, understood this and trusted it far more than if he had ideological or political motives. Even the Soviets found people suspect if they said they thought communism was the road to Utopia.

Hanssen gave the GRU our bugging techniques and operations. He let the Soviets know where the FBI was actively spending its money and gave them the FBI's list of suspected Soviet intelligence agents. He also compromised numerous human resources, including betraying Dmitri Polyakov, a CIA informant who rose to the rank of general in the Soviet Army. It's worth noting the Soviets did not arrest Polyakov until after he was betrayed a second time by CIA officer and Soviet spy Aldrich Ames in 1985.

The Soviets shot Polyakov in 1988 in a small, walled courtyard inside the Kremlin. That's the Kremlin for you. One-stop shopping.

In 1980, after only about a year of spying for the GRU, Hanssen's wife, Bonnie, caught Hanssen in the act when she walked in on him in their basement in Scarsdale, New York. She said he scurried to hide papers, but he was too late. He admitted to her that he was dealing with the Soviets, though he told her he was feeding them false information.

She didn't believe him, and she took him to their priest, Rev. Robert P. Bucciarelli, to confess. Bucciarelli first told Hanssen to turn himself in. The next day, the priest called Hanssen to say that he didn't actually need to turn himself in if he gave the money he'd received from the Soviets to a worthy charity and promised that he wouldn't do it again. Hanssen agreed to make monthly payments to the church as his retribution. . . . Yeah. Moving right along. . . . Some say Hanssen stopped spying for the Soviets for a while and then started up again. There is some debate about whether he stopped and for how long, but we know for certain he was spying for the Soviets again in 1985.

In 1981, the FBI transferred Robert Hanssen and his computer skills to headquarters in Washington, DC. Hanssen's task was budget management at first. Then, three years later, he was put on the Soviet team for the purpose of counterintelligence. Hanssen decided it was time to expand his list of clientele.

In an anonymous letter dated October of 1985, he wrote to the KGB requesting $100,000 in exchange for the names of three KGB agents that were informing to the FBI—Valery Martynov, Sergei Motorin, and Boris Yuzhin. Moscow took the deal.

The three Soviet spies had already been betrayed by soulless dirtbag Aldrich Ames, but Hanssen gave the KGB the confirmation they needed. The three agents were recalled to Moscow. Martynov and Motorin were executed. Yuzhin was sent to prison and was released on February 7, 1992, when Russian President Boris Yeltsin issued a general amnesty for political prisoners. Yuzhin did the smart thing and got the hell out of Dodge-ski. The FBI helped him resettle in the United States, and as far as we know, he is still alive at the time of publication of this book.

In 1987, the FBI attempted to discover if anyone in the Bureau had betrayed Martynov and Motorin. To do that, they reassigned Hanssen to Washington, DC, and put him on a project to study all of the known penetrations of the FBI, or, in other words, all of the people the FBI was investigating as possible double agents working for foreign countries.

Hanssen, of course, knew the answer to who betrayed the Soviet spies when he was given the assignment. He was the answer. Naturally, that was not the answer he gave the FBI. Before Hanssen turned in his study to the FBI in 1988, he turned over the entire project to the KGB, which let the KGB know who had been found, who had *not* been found, and the intelligence activities of other countries.

The following year in 1988, Hanssen slipped up again. While he and a team of FBI agents were debriefing a Soviet defector, Hanssen broke FBI regulations by revealing secret information to the defector. This violated the principles under which agents work when handling defectors. Agents are never looking to give defectors information. They're only looking to get information *from* defectors. This is a universal rule. Hanssen's co-worker reported him, but their boss let it go.

In 1989, the FBI was investigating State Department employee Felix Bloch, the director of European and Canadian Affairs for the State Department. Hanssen informed the KGB of the investigation. The KGB "cleaned" Bloch, or in other words, they warned

Bloch and cut off all contact with him. As a result, the FBI was not able to gather enough information to prosecute Bloch for treason. At least the State Department had seen enough from the FBI to fire Bloch and to deny his pension. The Bloch case further drove the suspicion that the FBI needed to look closer to home for the traitor, as it was yet another case where it was clear there had been a mole, and one that Aldrich Ames could not have influenced.

During that same time frame, Hanssen also turned over technical intelligence to the KGB, such as signal intercepts that the FBI was aware of from agencies such as the CIA and NSA. In addition, we now know that on two separate occasions, Hanssen gave the Soviets a complete list of Soviet double agents that were working for us. The double agents were all neutralized in one form or another, ranging from being sent to prison, getting whacked, or being "tripled back," i.e. turned into triple agents. It's worth noting that the Soviets' favorite way of killing double agents was to cremate them alive, feet first, one inch at a time. Hanssen had to have known this when he betrayed the agents.

In 1990, Hanssen's fellow FBI employee and brother-in-law, Mark Wauck, started making noise to the FBI about his own suspicions of Hanssen. Hanssen's wife, Bonnie, had innocently mentioned to Mark that Hanssen talked of retiring in Poland, which was part of the Soviet Eastern Bloc at the time he said it—not a place most FBI agents, or anyone else, would have considered retiring to at that time. Wauck also knew Hanssen had an unexplained pile of cash sitting unattended in his home. Wauck went to his own supervisor with his suspicions of Hanssen, and no action was taken on this second red flag.

A third red flag was that Hanssen bragged to close friends that he had secretly videotaped himself and his wife having sex. He even offered to show the tapes to some of his friends and co-workers.

Given that his wife was unaware of the tapes and not part of the bargain, it was a serious betrayal. When we juxtapose that with the fact that Hanssen was a champion recruiter for Opus Dei, it reveals an inexplicable anomaly in Hanssen's behavior. Again, for reasons unknown, the red flag was ignored.

The Soviet Union collapsed in 1991. After that, Hanssen didn't know how things would shake out in Moscow, and he was naturally worried about being exposed, so he broke off contact with the KGB. The KGB had its own upheaval, and KGB agents were working hard on their own survival—literally. They likely didn't pay much attention to Hanssen's change of heart or bother to blackmail him into continuing his work for them.

Then, in 1992, Hanssen decided he needed more cash and/or more ego gratification. This time, in a brazen act, he personally went to the Russian Embassy in Washington, DC, and approached the GRU to renew his services. The GRU thought it was a fake approach, or a "provocation," even though Hanssen told the GRU he was an FBI agent. The GRU, assuming Hanssen was there to screw them over, had the Soviet ambassador file an official protest with the US State Department. The Russians thought Hanssen was a triple agent because it was preposterous to them that a double agent would come back. The State Department notified the FBI. At this point, it should have been abundantly clear to the FBI that they had a major problem. However, nothing was done.

The following year, Hanssen was caught hacking a fellow agent's computer at the FBI. Hanssen pretended he was doing a test to show them that the system wasn't secure. His boss was not amused by the incident, but FBI management bought Hanssen's excuse. Again, nothing was done.

By 1994, it was abundantly clear to the Intelligence Community that there was at least one mole. The FBI stepped up their efforts and formed a joint task force to look for the traitor. While they missed Hanssen, the joint task force did uncover another spy, CIA officer Harold James Nicholson, as well as Nicholson's son, who were both convicted on espionage charges. Less fortunately, the task force also focused in on an innocent CIA officer by the name of Brian Kelley. Kelley was exonerated after an investigation and continued his career with the CIA, receiving the Distinguished Career Intelligence Medal for his service. The task force never did look at Hanssen as a suspect.

The tables started turning on Hanssen in 1994 after the arrest of Aldrich Ames. For many years, the leaks from Aldrich Ames and others had clouded the fact that Hanssen was leaking, as well. Both the FBI and the CIA knew there was at least one mole, but the FBI, with all-too-human bias, presumed that the leak was in the CIA and not inside their own organization. However, some of the leaks could not have come from Aldrich Ames. Combined with the fact that, after Ames was arrested, the leaks continued, the evidence became irrefutable. The FBI began looking in their own house.

Also in 1994, as a response to the CIA Aldrich Ames debacle, the National Counterintelligence Center was created in Washington, DC. Hanssen applied for a transfer to the new organization as a way of getting further into the nest. However, he was told he would need to pass a lie detector test for his application to proceed. Hanssen withdrew his application.

In another incident, Hanssen was caught red-handed with a password-cracking program on his computer that did not belong there. He had no need to have it, and he should not have had it. Security auditors impounded his computer, and an investigation was opened. Hanssen's excuse? He needed the program to get past the password requirement because he wanted to use the color printer. Fantastically, FBI leadership accepted his excuse.

Life went on quite sweetly for Robert Hanssen for many more years. To ensure that sweet life, he periodically ran searches in the FBI system to see if he was under any investigations. Those searches were more red flags that should have been easily spotted and set off alerts. Apparently, they were not. Once Hanssen was certain he was not under investigation, he went back to the Russians again.

In 1999, Hanssen directly contacted the Sluzhba vneshney razvedki ("SVR"), the Russian foreign intelligence service, to offer his services, and the SVR accepted. Hanssen renewed his business of selling information to the Russians. The whole time he was doing this, he was still routinely leaving footprints through the FBI computers.

All the while, Hanssen attended 6:30 a.m. mass every day, a habit of decades, and he annoyed other Catholics in the Bureau by telling them to go to mass more often. He also encouraged them to publicly denounce the Soviets as godless heathens. When not in his FBI office, attending daily masses, or servicing his dead drops, Hanssen was obsessing over internet pornography, frequenting DC strip clubs, or lavishing gifts on his stripper girlfriend of the couple years prior to his arrest. She claims he never slept with her, but that he instead continuously tried to convert her to Catholicism. . . . Enough red flags, yet?

Finally, in 2000, urgently seeking the mole, the FBI paid KGB agent Alexandr Scherbakov $7 million for a Russian file on the traitor. The amount is an indication of how upset the FBI was about this traitor, as the Bureau is almost as happy to hand over $7 million as a politician is to concede an election.

The file did not contain Hanssen's name, but it did contain a voice recording of Hanssen and a KGB agent. Investigators weren't sure who the voice belonged to, but they thought it sounded familiar. Eventually, they realized it was the voice of

Robert Hanssen. There were also fingerprints in the file that matched Hanssen's. Finally, the FBI put Hanssen under surveillance and confirmed that he was the mole.

To gather the evidence to prosecute Hanssen, the FBI set him up by creating a new position for him as the supervisor for FBI security. They gave him an assistant by the name of Eric O'Neill, who was there to watch Hanssen. O'Neill, an undercover surveillance specialist, was only twenty-seven years old—too young to be a special agent. He was also a newlywed and a freshly-minted college graduate going to law school at night. Both a Catholic and a computer geek—relating points with Hanssen—O'Neill was selected specifically for his youth and inexperience, as the FBI correctly guessed that Hanssen would not suspect the youth of being a plant.

O'Neill discovered that Hanssen was using a Palm PDA, and that it was virtually impossible to separate him from it. The FBI had evidence that Hanssen was about to do a "drop," which meant he was about to give the Russians more documents. They needed to get the information off of that Palm PDA. To get it, O'Neill arranged with Hanssen's bosses that they would surprise Hanssen and take him to the in-house gun range. While Hanssen was gone from the office, O'Neill downloaded the contents of Hanssen's Palm PDA. The FBI decrypted the files and had more than enough evidence on the upcoming drop. The final step was to catch the traitor in the act.

Hanssen, as an FBI agent, was hard to surveil both physically and electronically. He also apparently thought he saw signs of surveillance because he started looking for another job. However, he couldn't resist one more betrayal. Hanssen made arrangements to leave a packet of classified materials for the Russians at his favorite "dead drop," code named "Ellis," in Foxstone Park near his home in Vienna, Virginia. Hanssen went to the drop on February 18, 2001, and the FBI arrested him.

Hanssen is now Federal Bureau of Prison #48551-083. In other words, he is still rotting, preferably miserably, in the ADX Florence supermax prison near Florence, Colorado, serving out fifteen consecutive life sentences. He spends twenty-three hours each day in solitary confinement, which was his deal after a plea bargain. Federal prosecutors, along with countless individuals in the Intelligence Community, wanted the death penalty. We here at Bayard & Holmes, in a gesture of compassion, are starting a GoFundMe site to hire prison guards for Robbie that were trained at the Soviet Vorkuta Gulag so he can be surrounded by the people to whom he sold out his country.

Those in the Intelligence Community widely consider Robert Hanssen to be the most damaging spy in the history of the FBI, and some would say in the history of the United States. He spied off and on for the GRU and the KGB—later the SVR—for over twenty years. Over the course of more than twenty separate occasions, he passed the Soviets and Russians over two dozen computer diskettes and over six thousand pages of classified documents. In return, Hanssen received over $600,000 from the Soviets and Russians.

One might reasonably ask how he was able to operate for so long. That seems to be the question with every traitor, from the Cambridge Five to Boyce and Lee and from Manning to the US Navy officers involved in the Fat Leonard Conspiracy. Why didn't someone, especially the FBI, pick up on the clues?

There are almost always multiple facets to the answer. One facet is that Hanssen was clever. He never used drop sites that his Russian handlers picked, but instead picked his own to avoid Soviet and later Russian surveillance. He also always used indirect exchange methods for transferring information and cash, and in the decades that Hanssen sold information to the Soviets, he never personally met with them.

Another facet, though, can be put down to institutional bias. It is natural in any group to assume that bad apples are outsiders. All organizations can have a higher opinion of themselves than what is justified, and at times, that has been particularly true with the FBI. The vast majority of FBI agents are excellent agents and outstanding American citizens, and, for the almost one hundred years of the FBI's existence, they have consistently demonstrated courage, dedication, and sacrifice. As a result, the loyal agents tend to assume that other FBI agents are loyal Americans, as well, making it more difficult for the FBI to spot an enemy among their own. This bias is the good will that traitors trade on, and Robert Hanssen did so for decades.

And the official FBI position on Robert Hanssen? The Bureau is proud of itself for living up to its duty to catch the mole.

THE BOOTY

Anna Chapman
The Kremlin's Crimson Cupcake

Mata Hari
Seductress, Yes, But a Spy?

Giacomo Girolamo Casanova de Siengalt
Lover, Gambler, Doctor, Lawyer, Booty Spy

Isabella "Belle" Boyd
The Siren of the South

Hekmet Fahmy
The Fox Behind the Desert Fox

Amy Elizabeth Thorpe
The Spy Who Loved

Josephine Baker
From Homeless Child to Espionage Icon

19

BOOTY SPIES

IT IS OFTEN CLAIMED THAT THE OLDEST PROFESSION IS prostitution. We weren't there so we can't be sure, but if prostitution was the first paid profession, then spying might have been a close second, and depending on how it was done, it might also rate a "first profession" claim. The two professions have been linked from the start.

The goal of the booty spy is to use sex or sex appeal to obtain information or to get a target into a compromising position for the purpose of blackmail. Honeypots, a subset of booty spies which we address in our previous book, *Spycraft: Essentials*, have the specific task of getting their mark into a compromising sexual position as quickly as possible or to seduce them into revealing information. It's worth noting that the United States has never been as big on honeypots as other countries, such as Russia.

As we said, honeypots are only a subset of booty spies, as not all booty spies sleep with their marks. For example, some famous booty spies, such as Josephine Baker, were entertainers who were known for their risqué performances and sex appeal, and whose allure made them welcome among the elite.

Some booty spies are from the privileged classes, and some over-come destitution to rise to the top of their professions. Some are highly trained professionals, while others are well-placed amateurs using the gifts their mamas and papas gave them with the skill that comes naturally to many women and men. Some are among the best and the brightest, and some are just lucky. All show how vulnerable a substantial percentage of us mere humans can be when sex is used to spark our imaginations and to pry into our most vulnerable shadows.

20

ANNA CHAPMAN
THE KREMLIN'S CRIMSON CUPCAKE

INTELLIGENCE PROFESSIONALS MIGHT WONDER WHY WE INCLUDE Anna Chapman in a section with the likes of Belle Boyd and Josephine Baker. We would tell them it is for contrast to illustrate the point that even bad spies can do damage. While some booty spies are clever enough to succeed with minimal training, others can have the best training an enemy country can provide and still not be particularly clever. Nevertheless, it doesn't take a genius to extract information or blackmail material from a horny mark, and even a person with little talent at espionage can sometimes get useful work done. Anna Chapman is just such a booty spy . . . emphasis on the booty.

After the fall of the Soviet state, the KGB entered into a reorganization phase, being broken apart, relabeled, and shuffled about. Put generally and imprecisely, the KGB evolved into what is currently the Federal'naya sluzhba bezopasnosti Rossiyskoy Federatsii ("FSB"), which is the domestic intelligence service, the SVR, which is the foreign intelligence service, and a Committee for special programs that has more branches than Queen Victoria's family tree. Put specifically and accurately, the current

Russian security services are whatever Vladimir Putin wants them to be on any given day.

Vladimir Putin directly controls the FSB, the SVR, and all other security organizations from electronic surveillance to domestic law enforcement and domestic and foreign services. These organizations are Putin's vast private army that answer to no one but him. The people at the top these organizations see themselves as the "knights of Russia" and the modern nobility. Their families are appointed to high positions in the intelligence services or in Russian businesses such as communications, finance, and Russian media. It makes democracy in Russia structurally impossible.

The bottom line is that the organization of Russian security services is complicated and not as clear as our FBI, CIA, NSA, etc. We could write a detailed explanation of every transition in the Russian security services over the past thirty years, but life is short. Why spend it being miserable writing such a tome so that only a handful of other people could be miserable reading it? Most people would rather write or read a toaster warranty. We'll pass. Suffice to say it's complicated.

In 2010, the FBI executed a sting operation that started with netting ten Russian SVR agents spying in America. These spies' operation relied on simple hand-written ciphers, using standard middle-school level espionage techniques. The FBI had been onto the group for some time, but when one of them got too close to a high-level politician, it was time to roll them up. As there is still much embarrassment among top politicians about that, we sadly can't tell you which one got duped, but the spy was the Kremlin's Crimson Cupcake, Anna Chapman.

Our information on Anna's early life came from Russia, so take it with a grain of salt and remember that in most cultures of the world, truth telling is considered a form of mental illness.

According to the Russians, Anna Vasil'yevna Kushchyenko, a.k.a. Anna Chapman, was born Feb 23, 1982 in Volgograd. The Russians like to say her father was a big shot in the KGB, but he actually served in Nairobi, Kenya, which means he was about a medium shot. We think Anna had a typical KGB family upbringing, and that she was educated with other KGB children, participating in the Red Pioneers, Red Guards, party elite schools, and party propaganda. According to the Russians, she studied economics at Moscow University. There are all kinds of colorful rumors about Anna being an advanced sexual libertine at an early age, but there is no way to know if that is actually true or just gossip. That's basically all that we could dig up on her early life. Now, we'll go on to what we *actually* know that we did *not* find out from the Russians.

Anna visited the United Kingdom in 2002 and met her first husband, Alex Chapman, at a rave party at the docks in London. They married five months later. For the next four years, Anna worked for Barclay's bank and several other companies, and she and Alex split their time between residing in Russia and in the United Kingdom. The couple divorced in 2006.

After a brief residency back in Russia, Anna was sent to join the rest of the SVR team, which had slipped into the United States around 2000. Her task was to find and get next to US policy makers. To do this, she lived in Manhattan and ran her own real estate company, PropertyFinders, Ltd.

The PropertyFinders front was an "overnight" success, dealing in high-end international real estate. Anna's well-staffed office was one block off Wall Street in the financial district of Manhattan. A question that is reasonable to ask is who invested for her on the US side of the pond? We do not know the answer to that, but she made inroads into Wall Street businesses, and most of her marks were Wall Street types. A busy girl in her romantic enterprises, Anna hit the party circle of restaurants and clubs by night to cultivate even more intimate contacts. Let's just say she had many colorful evenings during her time in the United States.

As for the team as a whole, it's clear that the SVR management in Moscow didn't have much confidence in them to begin with. Otherwise, the SVR would not have sent the spies out with such a primitive communication system. Holmes pictures the old-timers having the conversation . . . "These fools aren't ready to go out, but they aren't doing any good here. Might as well send them out. Better not give them anything too sophisticated to play with, or they'll screw it up." The system the team was using was simple enough that if there was a screw up, they could easily recover without having to use any real skill to figure out where they went wrong and fix things. Moscow knew they were sending out the B Team. These were not elite agents and were nowhere near the caliber of agents that would have been sent at the zenith of the KGB.

The team lived down to expectations. They used burst transmitters, but their frequency and timing of transmissions was highly redundant—a basic no-no of spycraft. Also, on more than one occasion, they left their cipher codes in insecure locations. Holmes suspects the NSA picked them up rather quickly. The FBI was onto the team for several years, tracking them in Operation Ghost Stories before rounding them up in 2010.

As part of the sting, Anna knowingly accepted a fake passport from an FBI agent. After she did so, she got nervous, and she violated SVR security protocol by calling her KGB daddy, belying the notion that she is the high-end Bond type that the Russians like to pretend she is. Her father advised her that it was possibly a sting and told her to take the passport to a local police station and turn it in. She did, but it was too late. On June 27, 2010, Anna and nine of her cohorts were arrested for espionage against the United States.

It is possible there were several reasons the ring was busted. According to the Russians, Col. Alexander Poteyev, who ran the spy ring, was actually working for the United States and was responsible for the ring getting busted. Poteyev ran from Moscow right before the bust, but his absence was no hindrance to Russian military courts. Poteyev was convicted in absentia for high treason and desertion. Anna testified at his trial.

According to sources in the United Kingdom, the FBI had been watching the Russian team for quite some time, and when Anna got too close to one of President Obama's cabinet members, the FBI decided it was time to roll them up. However, officials from the US Department of Justice claim the real trigger for rolling up the group was that Anna's teammate, Cynthia Murphy, a.k.a. Lidiya Guryeva, had established a friendship with a close personal friend and major fundraiser of Hillary Clinton's.

Though the team did not conduct their communications with the best of protocol, there were several bright and effective spies in the group. Anna was not one of them. She was the nepotism case, and if placements were strictly on merit, Anna Chapman never would have been inserted into that group. The rest were a cut or two above her.

Anna was most active in the United States during her last year before being arrested. When the team was rounded up, it was caught so red-handed that rather than wasting time with the usual denials or claiming that the spies were all here for a charity affair to feed starving American children, the Russians instead turned the arrests into an espionage recruiting event. The whole team, rather than being publicly chastised for screwing up the operation, were lauded as heroes of the Russian intelligence community.

The Kremlin's Crimson Cupcake was sent home to much fanfare and celebrity as part of an exchange. It's worth noting that 2018 poisoning victim, Sergei Skripal, was part of that exchange, released from Russia with three other prisoners. Skripal settled in the United Kingdom, where he was the victim of an assassination attempt on the part of the Russians, proving there is more than one way to renege on a deal.

When Anna returned home, we are certain she had no idea whether or not she would be treated to a one-way tour of the Kremlin's execution courtyard. She was no doubt greatly relieved when Putin decided instead to use her as an espionage marketing tool. Anna was touted to the Russian people as a hero, put on the cover of Maxim magazine in her underwear with a gun, and punished by being forced to dine with Putin.

Still a UK citizen because of her first marriage, Anna tried to go back to the United Kingdom—a reasonable response to having dined with Putin. However, in a reasonable response on the part of the Brits, the United Kingdom revoked her citizenship. Even Azerbaijan declared her a *persona non grata* in 2013. Anna was stuck.

It appears she made the best of it by cultivating a high-profile career as a runway model and a TV host with her own show, *Mysteries of the World with Anna Chapman*. In her private life, she is reportedly a multi-millionaire, and she gave birth to a son in 2015. She remains mum about the identity of the father. It is interesting to note that her first husband, Alex Chapman, died in March of 2018. There are questions surrounding his death. We don't have the answers.

The Chapman case is an important indication of the state of affairs in the SVR in the first decade of the 21st century. As late as 2015, we were seeing sloppy tradecraft in communications, in compartmentalization, in the discipline of their agents overseas, and in their operational discipline. Unfortunately, after a long series of debacles from 1995 to 2015, the Russians are tightening things up again and are now using people who are more skilled, more self-disciplined, and more tightly managed.

Although Russia has improved its espionage operations on all levels, there are still examples of less-than-professional behavior in their ranks. For example, a Russian FSB graduating class in 2016 got over-excited about themselves and decided to party like they would never be promoted to public office. They procured, by hook or by crook, some black Mercedes luxury SUVs, and for their graduation celebration, they rode around town hanging out the windows, screaming, drinking, raising hell, and taking selfies to post on social media. The memes and videos got back to the FSB. The FSB was not amused.

Instead of sending the graduates out in the field anyway, some veterans of the Soviet intelligence community were calling for them to be hung as traitors. A couple of the youngsters quit or were fired, and the rest were dispatched to the Kamchatka Peninsula and Chukotka—not the most auspicious start for FSB academy graduates. Soviet veterans were saying they must have been recruited in insane asylums.

To be fair, unprofessional and even treasonous behavior occurs in every country's military and intelligence communities at times. One need look no further than the Fat Leonard Conspiracy in our own US Navy for that. Sadly, we can't send our own bad apples to the Kamchatka Peninsula or Chukotka. Professionalism and loyalty are ongoing struggles wherever fallible human beings are involved in espionage, which is everywhere.

The Anna Chapman case is not just an example of slipshod tradecraft and inadequate internal discipline on the part of the Russians. It also points out that even at a low point in Russian intelligence operations, they were still able to get significant work done against us. That means we are not as hard of a target as we should be. This has to do with how little the United Kingdom and the United States perceive Russia as a threat. In 1960, Anna Chapman would have been viewed with a great deal of suspicion, and she and her team would not have gained access to banks or cabinet members.

Anna and her cohorts, sloppy as they were, accomplished some successes against us for one main reason—because men are . . . men. Many men are sexually vulnerable creatures who will jump on any stray rat that wanders in and hikes her skirts. We are picking on men, in particular, because they are generally easier targets for booty spies. Sadly, this pathetic behavior is not just limited to civilians in the halls of Congress or the skyscrapers of Wall Street, but it is also an issue with some members of the military. The Fat Leonard Conspiracy is an epic example. To be clear, we don't blame Anna or any honeypots. We blame the idiots who fall on top of them.

Individuals like Anna Chapman capture attention because they are colorful enough to stir a media consumer's imagination. We're sure that many male observers' first impressions of the Anna Chapman Maxim magazine appearance included thoughts along the lines of, "Yeah, I would have done her."

Intelligence Community members likely tended to see her differently, but ego plays a part there, as well. Male spies might have thought something like, "Hmm, she is a spy, but she never would have fooled *me*. Politicians are such idiots."

Female spies might have thought "Ugh! Another one. . . . Those damned guys are too easy."

But the bottom line is that booty spies are still sent out because they still work.

As for Anna Chapman, she may have been welcomed home to Russia and paraded around as a respected professional, but she will never be trusted with any other meaningful responsibilities among the new Russian "nobility" in the Russian intelligence hierarchy. Her tales of how she wagged her tail will always remain her most important asset to her country.

21

MATA HARI

A SEDUCTRESS, YES, BUT A BOOTY SPY?

THE MOST FAMOUS FEMALE BOOTY SPY IN MODERN TIMES WAS A Dutch woman named Margaretha Geertruida Zelle. However, there is some disagreement as to exactly who she spied for, if she even spied at all, or if she was the unlucky scapegoat of embarrassed French generals. That she was a seductress is not in question.

We know what you're thinking. . . . How could anyone with such an unwieldy name take up a career as a seductress?

We can only guess that she must have been talented, and she was at least smart enough to find a better stage name—Mata Hari. Due to her real or imaginary exploits as a booty spy, "Mata Hari" is a household name that has endured for over a century. It is exactly that fame that results in her legend being one of the most difficult to recount with any certainty.

Margaretha was born in The Netherlands on August 7, 1876. Her father had been a successful hatter, and he invested his money in oil at the right time. As a result, he made a fortune and was able to indulge Margaretha. She developed a reputation for being as spoiled as a European royal.

Unfortunately for Margaretha, her father went bankrupt in 1889 when she was thirteen years old. Two years later, her mother died and she was parceled out to her godfather. He decided to send her to a school where she would be trained as a teacher so that she would be able to have a career and be independent. It was a reasonable plan, but Fate was not on board with it.

The Headmaster of the school became infatuated with Margaretha, and they apparently had sexual relations. At the time, fifteen-year-old girls were considered eligible for marriage, but even back then, headmasters of schools in The Netherlands were expected to refrain from hands-on sex education in the curriculum offered to students in their care. Scandal broke out, and, naturally, rather than delivering a sound beating to the headmaster and sending him for a prolonged swimming lesson in a handy Dutch canal, the school board booted Margaretha out of the school. It must have been quite an education for a teenager far from home, but not the education that her godfather had anticipated.

Margaretha went to The Hague to live with an uncle. A few years later, she answered a classified ad that sought a suitable female for marriage. The ad turned out to be a hoax. A friend of 38-year-old Dutch Army officer Rudolph McLeod had placed the ad as a joke, but the joke went further than the friend had perhaps intended. Eighteen-year-old Margaretha and Rudolph became engaged, and they were married on July 11, 1895.

The couple traveled to the Dutch East Indies and had two children. While in Indonesia, Margaretha studied Malaysian culture and trained as a dancer. Rudolph apparently studied drinking and spousal abuse. Also, not content with his pretty young wife, he kept a concubine. Margaretha and Rudolph's son died of poisoning when he was two years old. In 1902, the family returned to The Netherlands, and soon after, Margaretha and Rudolph separated.

Margaretha decided to start a new life and took a train to Paris. She used her knowledge of Malaysia to create an entertainment genre based on her version of Malaysian dance style. The dancing involved little clothing, lots of jewelry, and a few supposedly Malaysian phrases. There likely weren't many Malaysian speakers in Paris at the time, and serious dance critics were not her intended audience.

It worked. She was a huge sensation. Margaretha abandoned her burdensome name in favor of "Mata Hari," which means "sun" or "eye of the day" in Malay. She also created a new history for herself, leaving behind the orphaned child she was and claiming to be the daughter of a Malaysian princess and a Dutch baron.

Wealthy and influential European men couldn't get enough of Mata Hari. She was kept by multiple lovers, usually senior military officers and politicians, and she traveled extensively, making her an ideal tool for scooping up secrets. The French tried to use her to spy against the Germans. Some sources say the French offered her a million francs if she could seduce King Frederick Augustus III of Saxony, and others say the deal was to seduce the half-wit Crown Prince Friedrich August Georg. Mata Hari did, indeed, seduce Crown Prince Friedrich August, but we don't know if she got anything useful out of him. We're pretty sure she didn't get anything useful from the French, like the million francs. However, what Freddy Jr. lacked in military acumen and political skill, he made up for in cash, and he shared lots of it with Mata Hari. If spying was her goal, she had a good cover.

Cultural critics in Europe claimed she lacked dancing ability and was nothing more than an exhibitionist, but when the Crown Prince of Saxony opens his bank accounts, who cares what the critics say? Mata Hari had entrée to Europe's top social circles. She didn't need the critics. If anything, their scorn might have added to her appeal by making her something of a prized forbidden fruit. She was the sort of woman that wealthy sons tripped over when they were allowed out to play without adequate supervision.

The Netherlands was neutral during WWI, so with her Dutch citizenship, Mata Hari was able to travel freely through warring countries. However, her contact with senior military officers in France, Germany, and Belgium raised the suspicion of the British Secret Service. She traveled to England in November of 1916, where she was arrested in Falmouth and taken to London. Sir Basil Thomson, the assistant commissioner at Scotland Yard, interrogated her and released her. Mata Hari returned to France.

According to German records, she traveled to Madrid in late 1916 and met with the German military attaché, Major Arnold Kalle. She asked him to set up a meeting with her part-time lover, the crown prince, and claimed she could share some valuable intelligence about the Allies. We don't know if it was an empty claim to get next to the prince or if she actually gave him information.

On February 13, 1917, the French arrested Mata Hari at the Hotel Élysée Palace on the Champs-Élysées and accused her of spying. Unfortunately for Mata Hari and for historians, the investigation and the trial were conducted in secrecy. The French claimed that she had been responsible for the deaths of 50,000 French soldiers by revealing French plans to the Germans. Whether or not she actually spied for anyone has never been determined with anything approaching reasonable certainty. That lack of certainty didn't stop the French from convicting her of espionage. On October 15, 1917, they executed Mata Hari in Vincennes by a firing squad.

This is what we do know:

- Germany operated a highly successful intelligence service during WWI. It often anticipated Allied offensives and moved troops, artillery, and supplies to the right place at the right time. Eventually, Germany and its poorly-led Austrian pals ran out of troops and supplies and lost the war.

- Offensives on the Western Front were difficult to keep secret. Those fascinating new devices called "airplanes" and "airplanes with big cameras" made it difficult to hide tons of ammunition and supplies being amassed for offensives.

- No general can easily live with the blame for a failed offensive. Try to imagine being responsible for the deaths of thousands of young men and nearby civilians. Americans can remember the shock, horror, and disbelief at the loss of 2,977 victims of terrorism on 9/11. France and its generals had to accept the deaths of 1,400,000 soldiers and watch 4,000,000 maimed French soldiers try to survive with their wounds. Finding scapegoats was likely a tempting option.

- The head of French Counterintelligence, Georges Ledoux, was later arrested for being a double agent in the employ of the Germans. He was cleared of all charges. Was he working for the Germans? Would he have given up Mata Hari if she were a valuable spy for Germany? If it was his only viable option for keeping his own skin intact, he might have been willing to give her up. If she were *not* spying for the Germans, he certainly would have been willing to toss her to the wolves.

- While in British custody, Mata Hari confessed to

Scotland Yard interrogators that she was a French spy
working against the Germans.

- During her interrogation in France, Mata Hari claimed
  that she was a double agent working for France against
  the Germans.

Considering Mata Hari's difficult youth, it is possible that she was
simply being whatever she needed to be at any given moment to
survive. When she confessed to Scotland Yard investigators, she
may have been doing what had become a long habit—telling
people what she thought they wanted to hear.

We can only imagine how many times she told some depressed
French or German officer that she didn't know men were "so
large," or that she had never experienced physical fulfillment
before that night. She was likely well-practiced at the art of sweet
talk and was obviously adroit at soothing male egos. The collective weight of her lies might have inadvertently created a believ-
able image of a sophisticated spy. It is also possible that she was a
spy without any strong loyalty who responded to whatever
opportunity presented itself. It's anyone's guess.

The French sealed the files of the Mata Hari case for one
hundred years, but they opened the files early in 1985. The information in them left journalists convinced that she was innocent
of espionage. However, drawing conclusions from the French files
is tricky at best, as they could not possibly contain transcripts of
everything that Mata Hari said to German officials during her
visits to Germany.

We will likely never know for certain how much effective spying
Mata Hari did. Regardless of her actual career or lack of career in
espionage, she left us with an enduring archetype of the female
spies. If we were to write an accurate book about "women spies,"

it might not be easy to publish. It would contain far too many examples of boring secretaries, cleaning ladies, nurses, librarians, ministers' wives and the like. If nothing else, we owe Mata Hari a little gratitude for spicing up the spy business.

Now let's take a look at what the grown men and women of booty espionage can accomplish . . .

22

GIACOMO GIROLAMO CASANOVA DE SEINGALT

LOVER, GAMBLER, DOCTOR, LAWYER, BOOTY SPY

USUALLY, WHEN WE THINK OF SEDUCTION AS A TOOL FOR ESPIONAGE, we think of female seductresses like Mata Hari or Belle Boyd, but sex is a tool that also has been used, although less famously, by male spies. Of those spicy gentlemen, perhaps the most famous, was Giacomo Casanova de Seingalt, a booty spy who used his intellect, talent, mojo, and fame to gain access to the aristocrats of Europe on behalf of the Vatican and others.

On April 2, 1725, in Venice, an Italian actress by the name of Zanetta Farussi gave birth to a boy. She and her husband, Gaetano Casanova, named the boy Giacomo. Thanks to his parents' successful careers, Giacomo Girolamo Casanova de Seingalt had a comfortable childhood and received a good education. He was a bright and promising student.

When young Casanova was nine, his parents sent him to a boarding school in Padua, Italy. He didn't like the dormitory life and convinced one of the teachers, a priest named Abbe Gozzi, to take him home to live with Gozzi's extended family. According to Casanova, Gozzi's younger sister, Bettina, seduced him and frequently fondled him. Apparently, Bettina was at least as good a teacher as her brother, and she helped Casanova discover his true calling in life.

At age twelve, armed with his new skills, Casanova entered the University of Padua, where he graduated five years later with a law degree in spite of the fact that he said he would have preferred medicine. According to Casanova, the more outlandishly one performed as a doctor, the more they could charge their patients, whereas with law, in Italian courts, one had to at least appear to be competent in their profession.

While studying law, Casanova took it upon himself to study chemistry and medicine, as well, and he developed a reputation as a skilled amateur physician. Along with sex, law, and medicine, Casanova developed a less benign habit while in Padua—he became a compulsive gambler.

Thanks to his law degree, Casanova received an appointment as a Catholic priest of sorts. At the time, there were levels of vows depending on the intended church career path, and Casanova's vows were not stringent. He was a "canon," which is someone who is not ordained to perform the sacraments, such as taking confession or giving communion, but they can be an administrative specialist. They are officials of the church, but they have not taken vows of chastity or poverty.

While a canon, Casanova continued to travel to Padua for advanced studies. He demonstrated a skill for ingratiating himself with influential patrons, and in Venice, he befriended the powerful Senator Alvise Malipiero. The friendship served Casanova well until he developed an interest in the senator's young fiancé. The incident is instructive because it demonstrates Casanova's ability to establish trust with powerful men, along with his better-known ability to seduce women. It also reveals a touch of carelessness.

Venice was a conservative place at the time, but the city fathers encouraged the city's reputation as an eighteenth century Las Vegas. What happened in Venice, stayed in Venice. Wealthy tourists flocked there to enjoy the opportunity to behave more licentiously than they would at home, giving Casanova had plenty of opportunities for female company. His choice to risk losing the tremendous benefits afforded him by his friendship with the senator in exchange for an affair with one of so many available women speaks to his gambling addiction. The man loved risk.

Casanova left Venice and declined his mother's help in landing employment with powerful people. He preferred to make his own conquests. In Rome, he befriended the powerful Cardinal Acquaviva and became the Cardinal's personal scribe. He was well-liked in the Vatican and even gained access to the pope. However, a sex scandal arose, and Casanova ended up taking the blame.

The Cardinal politely convinced Casanova to leave the service of the church, and they supposedly parted as friends. It is possible that the entire matter was a ruse to provide cover for Casanova, and that Casanova remained in contact with the Vatican and continued to act as its agent. Unless the Vatican opens its records to the public, we shall never know for certain.

Casanova returned to Venice and purchased a commission as a major in the Venetian Army. He took leave of his regiment to make an unexplained trip to Constantinople for his old friend Cardinal Acquaviva. At age twenty-one, Casanova then sold away his army commission and took up work as a violinist. He happened to be riding in a gondola with a nobleman and senator of Venice from the wealthy and powerful Bragadin family when the senator suffered a stroke. Casanova rendered first aid by bleeding the senator and accompanied him to his palace.

The palace doctor decided to treat the senator with a mercury salve, but Giacomo realized that the mercury would kill the senator and had the attendants remove the balm. He took over treatment of the senator himself. The senator recovered, and Casanova acquired yet another useful alliance with powerful people, becoming the Bragadin family's legal counsel. However, he spent most of his time gambling and attending parties in search of his next seduction conquest.

Seducers beware! The seduced may not always be innocent. A scandal arose when Casanova was accused of rape, and although he was acquitted, he had to depart Venice. He decided to travel. Unfortunately, the details of this incident are obscured by history. If any inquisitive readers go to Venice and search through the court records from the 1700s, we'd love to know what you find on this.

In Parma in 1749, Casanova fell in love with a woman called Henrietta, the beautiful daughter of a well-connected nobleman in Provence, France. Her real name was Adelaide de Gueidan, and in his memoirs, Casanova describes her as his true love. Henrietta, on the other hand, apparently enjoyed Casanova's company, but did not think he was marriage material. In her, he had met his philandering match.

Henrietta was unhappily married and escaping her misery by entertaining love affairs and searching for her father. She was with a Hungarian officer when Casanova met her and whisked her away to Parma. He proceeded to fritter away his money trying to provide his love with a lavish lifestyle. He hired Henrietta a maid and an Italian language teacher, and he bought her a new wardrobe and a cello. In return, she was most ungrateful toward Casanova for his gifts, and when she found out where her father was in France, she left Casanova and made him promise that if they ever met again, he would pretend he never met her. In honoring that promise, Casanova used the name Henrietta to describe her when he wrote about her.

Having been jilted, Casanova set out to recover with a tour of France. In Lyon, he joined the Freemasons, thereby gaining entrance to yet more powerful groups. He moved on to Paris, where he spent two years studying French and adding to his reputation for affairs with powerful women. Then he traveled to Dresden to visit his mother. While there, he wrote a comedy play that was well-received.

Casanova's travels continued to Prague and Vienna, but finding their moral standards restrictive, he returned to Venice. Back in his home, he grew brazen in his affairs and amassed too many enemies. He was put on trial for being a Freemason and sentenced to five years in prison. However, after about six months, he escaped and fled to Paris.

In Paris, Casanova ingratiated himself in high society and enjoyed affairs with a variety of wealthy socialites. He even gained the favor of the French court by organizing a state lottery system, making tremendous commissions in the process. In addition to his skills in the bedroom and with the lottery system, he presented himself to members of high society as an accomplished alchemist, and he was in high demand as an alchemist and adviser to the powerful. He was a most useful man.

The French government decided to use Casanova and sent him to Dunkirk as a spy. After that, he accepted a mission to The Netherlands, where he succeeded in selling bonds to finance the French involvement in the Seven Years War.

Using his pay from these espionage endeavors, Casanova opened a silk factory, but he made the fatal mistake of employing young females. Any business endeavor that placed Casanova, twenty young women, and an abundance of silk all in the same location was bound to end in disaster. It did. He ignored his business, and the enterprise was soon reduced to his personal harem. He borrowed heavily and ended up in trouble yet again.

Casanova was imprisoned for his debt but released after a few days because of the intervention of one of his powerful French conquests, the Marquise d'Urfe. He sold his possessions and volunteered for another financial mission to Holland for the French government, but this time, he failed in his assigned task of selling bonds to Dutch banks. So Casanova did what any reasonable gambler would do—he traveled to Stuttgart, Germany and gambled away what remained of his fortune. Casanova was imprisoned again for debt, and again he escaped.

This time he fled to Switzerland, where he supposedly considered giving up his sex addiction in favor of a monastic life. He visited a monastery and returned to his inn to contemplate his future. However, upon returning to the inn, he discovered an attractive young woman, and his monastic plans went by the wayside. In an attempt to recover from the rigors of his few minutes of monastic lifestyle, Casanova went on a bit of a recuperative tour through Italy and France, renewing old friendships and completing more sexual conquests.

In 1760, Pope Clement XIII knighted Casanova in the Order of the Golden Spurs. It was not publicly explained why the Pope bestowed this high honor on the renowned playboy. Could it be that while he was in the sporadic employ of the French government, he was actually acting as a spy for the Vatican? It is not likely that the 18th century Catholic Church would award high honors to a man based on his sexual prowess.

Casanova returned to Paris and went to the same well one too many times. He obtained financing from the Marquise d'Urfe to arrange for occult powers to convert her into a young man. Eventually, she looked in the mirror enough times to realize that she was being duped, and she finally abandoned her role as one of Casanova's many guardian angels.

In 1763, Casanova traveled to England to try to sell the British government on the idea of a state lottery. The English were likely forewarned of his Vatican connection, and the government politely ignored him. However, his reputation and his inability to speak English did not seem to slow him down much in his social life.

Casanova eventually fell ill to what were likely multiple venereal diseases, and he left England. Then, his venereal diseases apparently in remission, he went on another wild tour of Europe, traveling from Belgium to Hanover, to Moscow, and back to Warsaw. In Warsaw, he met with Catherine the Great, but he was unable to bed her or sell her on his lottery scheme. Casanova was then expelled from Warsaw for fighting a duel over a young Italian actress.

Casanova's reputation began to weigh on him, and he was finding European aristocracy more resistant to his charms. He traveled to Spain to attempt to harvest new fields, but he had little luck there. Although officially exiled from Venice, Casanova went to work for the Doges as a spy. To facilitate this, the Doges once more granted Casanova safe passage to and around Venice in 1774. Casanova had always used his spare time to write and publish, and now that his life slowed down a bit in Venice, he translated the *Iliad* to Italian and published it. The book was a success.

Then life came full circle. Casanova heard that his first lover, Bettina, had fallen ill. He traveled back to Padua to see her one last time. She died in his arms.

Then, in 1779, at the age of fifty-four, Casanova fell in love with a kindhearted seamstress. She became his live-in lover. He complained of boredom in his settled life, but his publishing pace increased, and he wrote his autobiography, *The Story of My Life*.

In 1785, Casanova became the librarian for the Count Von Waldstein of Bohemia. Twelve years later, he was contemplating a return to Venice, but Venice vanished before he could make the trip. Napoleon had annexed it. Then, on June 4, 1798, at the age of seventy-three, Giacomo Casanova, the lover, gambler, writer, doctor, lawyer, and spy, spoke his last words. "I lived as a philosopher and died as a Christian." As with most espionage figures, he took his professional secrets with him to the grave.

23

ISABELLA "BELLE" BOYD

THE SIREN OF THE SOUTH

MEN COME WITH A THREE-SENTENCE MANUAL. . . . FEED ME. FEED my ego. Feed my libido. . . . Confederate spy Belle Boyd wrote the book.

During the American Civil War, espionage and counterespionage played critical roles in the progress of the conflict. The Confederate government was fighting with inferior numbers and material, and they intended to fight a largely defensive war. As such, they placed great importance on gathering intelligence about Union troop strength and positions. By remaining informed of Union Army dispositions and intentions, the Confederate military hoped to be able to remove troops from areas that were not under immediate threat of Union attack and concentrate them at the right place at the right time to thwart Union advances. As a result, the Confederacy was often successful in beating the larger Union Army to the punch.

The Union Army also engaged in intelligence operations, but since the Union strategy required the siege and capture of fixed positions within Confederate lines, there was generally less urgency in obtaining Confederate plans. For the most part, the

Union intended to take the initiative and render useless whatever plans the Confederacy might formulate. They believed that as long as the Union Army could maintain adequate pressure on multiple fronts, Confederate plans would not matter. They thought that once the Union Army decided to attack a Confederate position, the Confederate response would be predictable from the Union point of view.

With the exception of Lee's Gettysburg campaign, intelligence on troop strength and location was far more critical to the Confederacy throughout the American Civil War than it was to the Union Army. During his Virginia campaign, Ulysses S. Grant succinctly described basic Union strategy when he told his staff in a moment of disgust to "Stop wasting your God-damned time talking about what Bobby Lee might do to us and get busy figuring out what *we're* going to do to *him*."

With the urgent need for intelligence, the Confederacy was heavily dependent on its spies. One of the most famous and successful of these Confederate spies was a young Virginia woman named Isabella "Belle" Boyd.

Belle Boyd was born on May 9, 1844 to shopkeeper Benjamin Reed Boyd and his wife, Mary Rebecca Glen Boyd, in Martinsburg, Virginia, now part of West Virginia. She was known for being bright and headstrong. Once, when she was told she was too young to attend a party, she rode her horse into the middle of the event in her family home and said, "My horse is old enough, isn't he?"

Belle attended Mount Washington Female College in Baltimore and graduated in 1860 at age 16. She then spent a year on the Washington, DC, social circuit. Her time as a debutante apparently helped her refine her skills in charm and intrigue.

On July 3, 1861, Belle was working as a nurse in the Shenandoah Valley town of Martinsburg, Virginia, when the Union Army occupied the town. During the next day's Independence Day celebration, Union soldiers noticed a Confederate flag flying from Belle's home. When the troops confronted Boyd's mother, an argument ensued. According to Belle's memoir, the soldier "addressed my mother and myself in language as offensive as it is possible to conceive. I could stand it no longer." Belle shot and killed the Union soldier.

When a Union officer investigated the incident, he apparently fell victim to Belle's charm and forgot why the Union had brought an army to the Shenandoah in the first place, and why Union taxpayers had been kind enough to furnish him with a pistol and generous quantities of ammunition. He found her actions were justified and released her. His lapse in judgment was an expensive one for the Union Army.

When the Union Army occupied Front Royal in 1862, Belle was well placed to operate as an "agent of opportunity." Her father, now fighting in Stonewall Jackson's Brigade, owned the best local hotel, and Belle found herself surrounded by Union officers. She successfully used her charm and eavesdropping skills to obtain useful information from the Yankees as they pored over maps and debated strategy at their hotel headquarters. She also used female messengers, including slaves, to deliver written information to Generals Stonewall Jackson and Turner Ashby.

During the Shenandoah Valley campaigns, Jackson's brigade earned the nickname "foot cavalry" because of their speed of march. However, moving fast only helps if one is moving in the right direction. Jackson and Ashby were in large part successful because they knew where to go and when to go there, and much of that information likely came from Belle Boyd. Jackson later publicly acknowledged Boyd and made her a captain and honorary aide de camp. Had that Union officer shot Belle on July 4th of 1861, Richmond might have fallen early in the war without the bloody campaigns that were fought in Virginia over the course of the following four years. However, at least a few less-gullible Union Army officers were suspicious of Boyd and placed her under surveillance.

On July 29, 1862, Belle was arrested and taken to the old capitol prison in Washington, DC. She used her most lethal weapon to gain her escape. She charmed her jailors and got herself released in a prisoner exchange program, to be "exiled to live with relatives." How stupid was that? We can only assume that she was a remarkably charming woman.

The press became enamored of her as well, dubbing her "Cleopatra of the Secession," "La Belle Rebelle," "Siren of the Shenandoah," and the "Rebel Joan of Arc." In spite of her celebrity, Boyd continued to operate spy networks and was arrested again in 1863. So now an embarrassed Union Army shot her, right? No. They released her because she was supposedly suffering from Typhus.

We know what you're thinking. . . . Why would Typhus interfere with the execution of a captured spy?

So glad you asked, but we got nothin'.

After being released from her jail deathbed, Belle underwent a miraculous recovery and returned to work. The Confederate government sent her to England on a blockade runner, *Greyhound,* as a messenger for the Confederate Secret Service branch operating out of the friendly confines of London. On May 10, 1864, Union Navy ships intercepted the *Greyhound*, and Boyd was captured red handed with plenty of incriminating documentation. US Navy officer Samuel Hardinge was placed on board the

Greyhound as prize captain and ordered to sail her and her captives to a US port.

Normally, this would be the part of the story where the captured spy is hanged from the yardarm. Forget it. Captain Hardinge fell in love with Belle and, naturally, she escaped with her skin intact. Samuel Hardinge, on the other hand, was jailed for allowing her to escape. Belle traveled to London from Canada and gave birth to Hardinge's daughter. She claimed to never have seen Hardinge again, but some historians believe that he joined up with her in England after three years in jail.

Later in life, Boyd returned to the United States and gave talks about her espionage career and on the need for reconciliation between the North and the South. Ironically, she frequently found herself in a reverse role from her Civil War years. Having spent the war trying to convince any fool that would listen that she was innocent of spying, she now had to spend her time convincing people that she was, indeed, Belle Boyd the spy.

During her absence from the United States, a cottage industry of Belle Boyd impersonation had sprung up. Journalists and historians had met so many Belle Boyd impostors that they had difficulty believing the real one when she did appear. On June 11, 1900, nature did what no Union officer had had the sense to do nearly four decades earlier. Belle died of a heart attack in Wisconsin during a speaking tour.

If Holmes had been a Union soldier, he gladly would have shot Belle. Several times. But he always gives credit where it is due. For a 17-year-old girl with so few resources to embark so decisively on an espionage career and survive so many captures is a remarkable accomplishment. So remember, guys, there's a time to use your gun, and a time to use your pistol. Don't ever confuse the two, or a lady like Belle Boyd will school you to your detriment, and perhaps to the detriment of your country.

24

HEKMET FAHMY

THE FOX BEHIND "THE DESERT FOX"

THERE IS A STEREOTYPE THAT MEN ARE EASILY MANIPULATED BY SEX, and that women often only have to show up naked to take advantage of that vulnerability. Egyptian bellydancer Hekmet Fahmy is a great example of why some would say that stereotype is based in fact. A well-placed booty spy does not have to be well trained to make a huge impact, and during WWII, German Field Marshal Erwin Rommel placed Hekmet right in the path of the British.

On June 10, 1940, Italy declared war on the United Kingdom. At the time, the United Kingdom lacked the resources to invade Italy, and Italy had no intention of invading Great Britain. However, the two enemies, along with France, had large colonial holdings in North Africa. At the time, the Suez Canal in Egypt was critical for the United Kingdom to connect the British Isles, Gibraltar, and Egypt to its colonial holdings in India, Ceylon, and Burma. Italian Dictator Benito Mussolini was confident that his forces, along with his German allies, could deal a major blow against the British from their bases in Libya, and perhaps threaten the British Suez Canal.

In general, the North African campaign of WWII is remembered as a series of battles. The United Kingdom dealt a decisive blow against the Italians in Libya. Germany sent reinforcements led by Field Marshal Erwin Rommel, a.k.a. the Desert Fox, who pushed the British back to the Egyptian border. Newly-appointed British Commander Field Marshal Montgomery led UK forces in a series of counterattacks. Those attacks were marginally assisted in the final phases by American landings in Morocco and Tunisia.

Conventional analysis of these battles emphasizes the skills of the opposing leaders. More in-depth descriptions also consider the logistical nightmares that both sides faced during the campaign. However, these assessments are based on well-researched analysis that was conducted without the benefit of certain classified information that was not released before 1970. When we consider the newer information, we learn that Erwin Rommel's tactical genius and Bernard Montgomery's inspiring leadership were heavily impacted by a variety of intelligence operations conducted by both sides.

Until July of 1942, the Desert Fox, enjoyed a tremendous advantage over the British in the form of timely, detailed, and accurate intelligence about British dispositions, supplies, and intentions. This information came inadvertently from US General Bonner Fellers.

General Fellers was the US liaison with the British in North Africa. Over his objections, he was instructed to use the US diplomatic "Black Code," a.k.a. Military Intelligence Code No. 11, to transmit messages to the US Joint Chiefs of Staff. Unfortunately, the Italians stole and copied that code from the US Embassy in Italy in September of 1941, prior to the US entry into the war. As a result, Rommel's staff read every word Fellers sent back to Washington before Washington read it. When Fellers was replaced in July of 1942, his replacement was permitted to switch his communications to US military ciphers. The Germans could no longer decipher the intercepted transmissions.

They turned to an Egyptian dancer for help. In the spring of 1942, a team of elite German commandos set out from Libya in US military vehicles that they had captured from the British. Their goal was to infiltrate two Abwher agents, Johannes Eppler and his radio operator, Hans Sandstede, into Egypt. Eppler had a German mother and an Egyptian father and had spent most of his childhood in Alexandria and Cairo. He was thoroughly trained and prepared for an operation in Egypt.

After a grueling fifteen-day trip through the desert, Eppler and Sandstede were dropped near the British Egyptian rail station at Asyut, Egypt. The two German spies made their way to Cairo where they used well-forged documents and high quality counterfeit British cash to rent a house boat and set up operations. The fate of Eppler's plans came down to one roll of the dice. He contacted an ex-girlfriend by the name of Hekmet Fahmy.

Hekmet Fahmy, born in 1907, was the niece of actress Aziza Amir. In the 1920s, she began her career with Ali El Kassar's theater group. Within a few years, Hekmet was the most famous and sought-after dancer in Cairo. During the course of her career, she would dance for numerous heads of state, including Adolf Hitler, Winston Churchill, the King of Greece, and Franklin Roosevelt. She also performed in movies, including The Will (1932) and Rabab (1942).

By 1942, Hekmet had access to the best night clubs and parties attended by the elite of local British and Egyptian society. She was the most alluring female celebrity in that country and enjoyed popularity with dance fans across Europe. She was also trusted in the highest military and social circles.

Not only did Fahmy spy for Eppler, she recruited other popular belly dancers to assist, allowing Eppler to operate one of the most successful honey traps of all time. British officers and government officials mistakenly trusted Fahmy and revealed critical information. As Fahmy's guests slept in her arms, Eppler searched their personal effects. By keeping track of which British officers from which regiments frequented the clubs, the Germans determined when particular units were being dispatched to the front. In some cases, the British officers and civilians revealed more-detailed classified information that was then transmitted to Rommel's headquarters. In effect, the Germans replaced an American general with an Egyptian bellydancer.

Thanks to the continued flow of quality intelligence, the Desert Fox confounded British attacks with timely delaying actions and skillful withdrawals. Rommel's tanks were outnumbered by now, but he could continually place them and their accompanying 77mm anti-tank guns in ideal locations to deal with British movements.

After a few months of operations in Cairo, the British pushed back the Afrika Corps from El Alamein. Communications with Rommel's headquarters became difficult. Eppler sought out the Egyptian Free Officer Corps, who were anti-British, to request assistance with passing information to Rommel. The young Egyptian officer who agreed to help was the future president of Egypt, Anwar Sadat.

In his 1957 book *Revolt on the Nile*, Sadat depicts Eppler and Sandstede as being lazy and overly-concerned with pursuits of the flesh. The depiction may have been unfair, as Eppler needed to appear to be a Scandinavian-American playboy in order to conduct his operations most effectively. If Eppler was in fact lazy, then we have to say that he was also fantastically lucky in his recruitment of Fahmy and his skillful use of her connections in gathering vital intelligence for the Desert Fox.

While Fahmy seduced British officers and Eppler fed their information to the Germans, the British simultaneously read and partially decrypted German military communications. They quickly became suspicious that German spies were succeeding in operations against them in Cairo. Either by managing too many local agents without insulation from themselves, or possibly because an Egyptian messenger was compromised, the British captured Eppler, Sandstede, and Fahmy.

With the defeat of the German intelligence operations in Cairo, combined with an increasing flow of Allied supplies and continued decryption of German military communications, the British were able to roll back Rommel across Africa. When the British captured 130,000 Germans in Tunisia in May of 1943, Rommel was on medical leave in Germany.

Rommel was tasked with organizing the German defenses on the French Atlantic Coast. However, he was implicated in a plot to kill Hitler. He committed suicide in exchange for his family being spared from persecution. The Nazis kept his betrayal of Hitler secret, announcing the Desert Fox had died of a heart attack. They gave Rommel a hero's funeral.

Eppler and Sandstede were sentenced to death as spies, but Egyptian King Farouk intervened, and their sentences were commuted. They were released from prison after the war, and Eppler became a successful construction engineer.

Fahmy was assumed to be an unwitting accomplice, and she was sentenced to two and a half years in jail. After her release, she was unable to revive her career, as the younger dance stars Taheya Carioca and Samia Gamal had taken the night clubs by storm in her absence. Hekmet turned to cinema and managed a few minor movie roles before investing the last of her money in her own production, *Al Moutasharide*. It failed miserably. The Egyptian Fox who did so much to aid the success of Desert Fox Field Marshal Erwin Rommel then turned to Christianity for solace and spent long hours praying in church. In 1974, she died at the age of sixty-six.

The North Africa campaign of WWII will always be remembered as a battle of supplies and opposing wits. It was, but it was also a campaign greatly impacted by the intelligence operations of both opponents. For a while, the balance of it all was tipped by the weight of a single untrained belly dancer.

25

AMY ELIZABETH THORPE
THE BOOTY SPY WHO LOVED

THE OPPOSITE OF MATA HARI WAS A MORE OBSCURE, BUT FAR MORE professional, intelligence legend Amy Elizabeth Thorpe. Skilled, focused, and loyal, she dedicated her substantial intellect and talent to her work with both MI-6 and the OSS during WWII. She knew what she was about and she didn't forget her goals, even when she crossed the lines.

A primary rule of intelligence work is that one must not mix love and work when dealing with any intelligence target. If an agent develops genuine affection for a target, the relationship can become dangerous to one or both of them. In wartime, this rule is even more critical, and if the agent is operating in hostile territory, the rule of avoiding romance is paramount. In spite of that, Amy Elizabeth Thorpe Pack Brousse broke this essential rule in wartime and lived to tell.

Thorpe was born in Minneapolis, Minnesota, on November 22, 1910. Her father was a US Marine Corps officer, and her mother was the daughter of a US senator. Amy's father made sure that Amy was well-traveled and educated about foreign cultures. Her mother made sure that she acquired training in the important social graces a woman needed to marry well. The combination laid the foundation for a successful career in the dangerous field of espionage.

Along with a suitable education, Amy had a bright mind. When she was eleven, she published a romance novel titled *Fioretta*. The book was set in Italy, and the protagonist was a beautiful young girl with a fantastic singing voice who used her talents and charms to free her unjustly imprisoned father. At eleven, Amy likely did not envision that *Fioretta* would one day help her in an intelligence operation.

When Amy was a teenager, her family moved to Washington, DC. While there, she met one of her admiring readers. That particular fan also happened to be an Italian naval officer by the name of Alberto Lais. Lais, serving at the Italian Embassy as a naval attaché, developed a platonic relationship with Amy and referred to her as his "Golden Girl."

At eighteen, Amy was considered one of the most charming and beautiful young women in the District of Columbia. Unfortunately, she was also a touch impetuous. She began an affair with an English diplomat by the name of Arthur Pack, who was nineteen years older than she was. They entered into an ill-conceived marriage, and in doing so, Amy gained British citizenship. Five months after their wedding, Amy gave birth to a healthy baby boy, proving what Piper's granny always said, "The first baby comes any time after the wedding. The rest take nine months." Amy and Arthur gave their first child to a foster family. They then had a second child, a baby girl, who Amy turned over to nannies.

In 1936, Arthur Pack was transferred to Madrid, Spain. Spain was on the verge of civil war, and as soon as Amy and Arthur arrived, Amy became involved in dangerous liaisons with the Nationalist movement. When the Spanish Civil War broke out in July of that year, Amy began smuggling rebel Nationalists caught in Republican-held territory to safety.

Amy also worked with the International Red Cross to transport supplies to Franco's Nationalist forces. When the British diplomatic staff and their families in northern Spain were trapped in a combat zone, Amy coordinated a rescue conducted by the British Royal Navy. Eventually, Amy's position was compromised when she was accused by a jealous woman of being a double agent for the Republicans. Amy left Spain.

In the fall of 1937, accompanied by her young daughter and a nanny, Amy traveled to Warsaw to work for the British intelligence services. At the time, Poland was still neutral and was an important intelligence target for France, Britain, Germany, and the Soviet Union.

Amy was fortunate in both her professional and personal lives while she was in Poland. On the personal side, her unsuitable husband, Arthur Pack, informed her that he was in love with another woman. Amy had to be thrilled at the news. Arthur then became ill and returned to England. On the professional side, Amy established close relations with young Polish patriots.

Poland had been successful in obtaining commercial copies of the German Enigma coding machine and had done valuable mathematical work in breaking German codes. Amy was able to target important Polish government officials with access to Poland's code-breaking operations on behalf of the British.

Though these officials were usually married and practicing conservative Catholics, neither their marital status nor their religion were defenses against Amy's charms. She used her friendly contacts to meet these officials at social events. Then she efficiently moved the new acquaintances from "hello" at the dinner table to "I love you" in her bed. The beautiful and brilliant Amy was one of the most successful honeypot operators in espionage history.

Some historians argue that Amy's contributions in capturing Poland's Enigma work were minimal. Polish patriots did, in fact, later smuggle out an Enigma machine to England after the Nazis invaded Poland. However, Amy's work at the very least allowed the British to begin organizing their code-breaking efforts against the German Enigma system earlier than they otherwise would have, and the value of that should not be underestimated.

Amy traveled to Prague and quickly penetrated the German diplomatic community, obtaining conclusive proof of Hitler's plans to dismember Czechoslovakia. Then, in the fall of 1938, the British ambassador ordered Amy to leave the country. One must wonder if Amy's departure from Prague was based on the usual friction between diplomats and spies operating under diplomatic cover, or if Amy's estranged husband had used his professional connections to have Amy sent back to England. Regardless of the reason, Amy returned to England and momentarily reconciled with Arthur Pack, who had regained his health. Then, in April of 1939, Amy and Arthur traveled to Santiago, Chile, where he served as the British commercial attaché.

When the United Kingdom entered WWII in 1939, Amy was writing political articles for Spanish- and English-language news-papers in Chile. At the same time, Britain was doing its best to improve its intelligence and propaganda efforts in the Western Hemisphere.

In 1940, the United Kingdom's Western operations were placed under the leadership of a proficient Canadian named William Stephenson. Stephenson, like so many other men, quickly devel-oped a strong liking for Amy. Amy left her husband in Chile and went to New York to work with Stephenson. Stephenson assigned her the code name "Cynthia" and sent her to the then-neutral capitol of Washington, DC. She was given the cover of a jour-nalist and ordered to target the Italian naval cryptologic system.

Amy immediately contacted her old literary fan, Alberto Lais, who by then was an Admiral in the Italian Navy and the Senior Italian Naval Attaché to the United States. According to MI-6's version of the story, Amy quickly charmed the 60-year-old admiral out of his uniform, his naval codes, and Italy's plans for scuttling any Italian ships in US ports when the war started. According to Amy, Admiral Lais was disillusioned with Mussoli-ni's drift toward Nazi Germany, and he and other members of his staff openly cooperated with her. According to the late admiral's family and the Italian Ministry of Defense, Amy and MI-6 are fabricators, and the admiral passed no information to anyone. In any event, the information found its way to British Admiralty hands and contributed significantly to the United Kingdom's many successes in the Mediterranean Theater.

By now, most booty spies would have considered themselves lucky to be alive and ready to be put out to pasture, but Amy, renowned for conquering hearts and libidos, was only getting started. After the Nazis completed their conquest of France in June of 1940, the United States remained neutral. Along with a few other Americans, Amy Elizabeth Thorpe did *not* remain neutral.

The Nazi-controlled Vichy French government, led by Marshal Philippe Pétain, was strongly anti-British while trying to maintain commerce with the United States and other neutral nations. Most of the French military and government officials who were serving in French colonial positions and French embassies around the world remained in their positions and formed the collabora-tionist Vichy government. However, Pétain's new government could not effectively realign the personal allegiances of all of its civil servants and military personnel overseas. While those indi-

viduals officially remained loyal to the French government, many
of them felt that they could best remain loyal to France by overtly
or covertly opposing the Vichy administration. This created a
sudden windfall of opportunities for the UK intelligence services
and their sympathizers in the United States, and Amy Elizabeth
Thorpe-Pack had the perfect set of talents to identify anti-Vichy
French patriots and exploit their predicaments.

Amy, or "Cynthia" as she was now known to MI-6, didn't waste
any opportunities. Agent Cynthia took on the cover of an American journalist and directly contacted the Vichy embassy in
Washington, DC. In May of 1941, she met the French Press
Attaché Charles Brousse and quickly guessed that he was not an
enthusiastic servant of the Vichy government. The fact that the
forty-nine-year-old Brousse was married to his third wife and
that he was a sophisticated "Don Juan" type did nothing to
dissuade Cynthia. Brousse had met his match.

How long it took Brousse to realize that he was the pigeon rather
than the hawk in his latest conquest is anyone's guess. It didn't
matter. He was in love with Amy and not in love with the collabo-
rationists that ran what was left of France. Brousse quickly began
cooperating directly with Amy in her intelligence work against
the Vichy government.

While outmaneuvering the Vichy government when it was so
riddled with anti-Vichy French patriots might have been easy,
Amy faced a more serious foe in Washington, DC—the FBI. FBI
Director J. Edgar Hoover took his orders from President
Roosevelt, but on matters of foreign policy, Roosevelt and his
cabinet members never trusted Hoover. Hoover was a staunch
isolationist. He was aware that the United States was operating a
privately-funded, expanding intelligence war against Nazi
Germany that was, at the time, without congressional approval,
and he didn't like it one bit. In particular, he didn't like it that he

wasn't running the operations. Hoover considered the "new breed" of intelligence operatives to be a threat to his power in Washington, and he used the FBI to try to foil them.

Amy was bold in action. She simply moved into the same hotel where Charles Brousse and his wife lived, and she used good field craft to overcome FBI wire taps and surveillance without running afoul of Brousse's spouse. By July of 1941, Amy was confident enough in her relationship with Brousse to request his help in obtaining the French naval cipher system without alerting the Vichy government.

Brousse explained to Amy that the code system was tightly guarded, and that only two people had access to it. He explained that he was not in the confidence of the cipher clerk or his assistant, and that they were staunch Vichy loyalists. When Amy suggested a nighttime burglary to access and copy the ciphers, Brousse explained that it would be impossible because they were locked in a heavy safe each night, and the area was patrolled by an armed guard accompanied by a guard dog.

At this point, it became evident that President Roosevelt was aware of MI-6's scheme to get the French codes. Bill Donovan, Roosevelt's head of the fledgling US Office of Strategic Services, provided Amy with a skilled safe cracker. Brousse informed the security guard that he would be using his office at night to have an extra-marital affair, and he gave the guard a small bribe to keep quiet.

Amy and Brousse started using the embassy for regular love making, and the guard got comfortable with the arrangement. One night, they gave the watchman some spiked champagne, and the safe cracker went to work. After much effort, the OSS safe cracker eventually opened the safe, but there was not enough time to safely remove, copy, and replace the books. They had to suspend their attempt.

Amy and Brousse made a second attempt with new safe information and the supposed combination, but without the safe cracker, Amy could not open the safe. On a subsequent night with the safe cracker in tow, they tried a third time.

When Amy sensed that the guard had grown suspicious, and that he was approaching the office where they were supposed to be in an act of love rather than an act of burglary, she quickly undressed and told Brousse to play along. Sure enough, the guard entered the office. Fortunately, they appeared to be doing something more natural and common than espionage, so the guard apologized and left. Amy, Brousse, and the OSS safe cracker were then able to get the codes copied and properly placed back into the safe. We now know that the United States and the United Kingdom were simultaneously running other operations to obtain the French naval and diplomatic codes. However, Amy at the very least verified the accuracy of the information.

Fortunately, the same code system was still in use during the US-led invasion of Northwest Africa in November of 1942. The United States and the United Kingdom were thus able to conduct their operations safe in the knowledge that the French Navy in Morocco, Tunisia, and Algeria would offer less than full resistance to the invasion. Most of the French in North Africa simply wanted to make enough noise to avoid further Nazi action against the French homeland.

After the Japanese attack on Pearl Harbor in December of 1941, the United States declared war against Japan. In turn, Nazi Germany and Mussolini's Italy declared war on the United States. Amy continued to work for both British MI-6 and the US OSS.

During an interview after the war, Amy was asked if, as a woman from such a respectable background, she was ashamed of her libertine activities in her espionage efforts. Amy laughed and pointed out that both the US OSS and British MI-6 assured her that her efforts had saved the lives of thousands of Allied soldiers and sailors and that "Wars are not won by respectable methods."

After the war, Amy's nominal husband, Arthur Pack, committed suicide. Charles Brousse and his wife divorced, and Amy Thorpe married her former pigeon. They lived in a castle in France, and by all accounts, the old spies were genuinely in love and happily faithful to each other. In 1963, Amy Thorpe Brousse died of cancer. Charles Brousse died ten years later when his electric blanket short-circuited and set the castle on fire.

It is rare for an agent employing honeypot methodology to last so long in the field after targeting even one high-profile pigeon. Amy was not only successful with multiple high-profile targets while working in dangerous areas like Poland and Czechoslovakia, she also eluded the FBI while conducting a major operation in Washington, DC, at the same time being emotionally involved with the operation's target. She was, in short, miraculous. Much of her early work with MI-6 still remains hidden in the past, but from what we do know, she was, without doubt, one of the bravest and most productive Allied agents of the WWII era.

26

JOSEPHINE BAKER
FROM HOMELESS CHILD TO ESPIONAGE ICON

WE OFTEN EXPECT OUR MILITARY HEROES TO COME EQUIPPED WITH great athletic prowess and years of grueling training. A few ultra-modern, nearly-magic gadgets and good looks don't hurt either. Josephine Baker showed up with one of the four. A brilliant and talented lady, she overcame her troubled beginnings, her lack of formal training, and the racist attitudes of the times to become both an international entertainer and an organizer of espionage and sabotage operations in France during WWII.

On June 3, 1906, Freda Josephine McDonald was born in St Louis, Missouri. She was the daughter of a black American washer-woman, Carrie McDonald, and, according to her foster son Jeanne-Claude Baker, her father may have been a white German-American for whom her mother had worked. Early to know a hard day's work, Josephine went to work for a wealthy white family as a washer girl at the age of eight. According to her biography, the women of the house purposely burned her hands for using too much soap on the laundry.

When Josephine was twelve, she quit school and became home-less. She lived in cardboard boxes and scavenged food from trash to survive. Is it possible anyone who saw her scrounging for food in the alleys of St. Louis imagined that she would someday do great service to the Allied armies and the people of France during WWII?

At the age of thirteen, Josephine obtained a job as a waitress, and she married one of her customers, Willie Wells. By the time she was fifteen, she had earned a reputation as a talented dancer, and she was able to support herself. She left Wells and quickly rose to the top of the Vaudeville dance circuit, spending the next six years entertaining American audiences.

In 1921, Josephine married American Willie Baker. Though she eventually divorced him, she kept his name for the rest of her life.

Josephine traveled to Paris in 1925 to perform for enthusiastic audiences. She was an instant celebrity. France fell in love with Josephine, and Josephine fell in love with France. She enjoyed greater integration in Paris than she could at home in the United States, and she expanded her career to include movie acting, singing, and song writing. According to Ernest Hemingway, she was the most exciting woman in Paris.

In 1935, Josephine returned to the United States to tour with the Ziegfeld Follies stage show. She had grown accustomed to something close to racial equality in France, and when she failed to "keep her place" in the United States, she generated mixed reviews. She returned to France in 1937 and soon thereafter married a Jewish French Industrialist named Jean Lion. By marrying Lion, she acquired French nationality.

As WWII approached, the French government contacted Josephine and asked if she would report on any interesting information that she picked up while attending parties, including some at European embassies. Josephine agreed. She quickly developed a skill for charming many fascist big wigs, who were desperate to cultivate an appearance of culture by being seen with her.

Josephine never attended any formal, longterm training program in espionage. However, when Germany invaded France, the French gave her brief emergency instruction in spycraft and taught her to use invisible ink and make safe information passes. During the Nazi occupation, Josephine was a prized commodity for parties and events held by Nazi and Italian fascist big shots. She was allowed to travel in and out of Vichy, France, Nazi-occupied France, and neutral countries such as Portugal and Switzerland.

She set up a theater and stage company in Marseilles, France and used it as a cover for a large espionage and sabotage organization. Refugees from Belgium and occupied France were taught to pose as stage artists, and the stage artists were taught to perform as spies. Her seemingly harmless musicians and actor types formed a valuable branch of the French Resistance.

In 1941, Josephine was stricken with a bad case of pneumonia. She and some of her recruits traveled to North Africa seeking a dryer, warmer climate. Free French leader General Charles De Gaulle and his staff felt that Josephine had done more than her share and encouraged her to remain safely in French Colonial Africa to recover her health. Josephine was devoted to the cause of freedom, and instead of remaining safe, she traveled to Morocco and set up an expanded espionage operation.

From her base in Morocco, Josephine safely traveled back and forth to Spain to communicate with Allied agents. She was able to assist the badly-outnumbered US OSS agents in Europe in setting up improved communications. Josephine apparently was warned to keep her distance from the OSS because it was known that a mole was loose in their European operations. She had to know that she was taking a tremendous personal risk by working with both the multiple branches of the French Resistance and agents of the OSS. Whatever risk she sensed, it did not slow her down.

Josephine suffered a miscarriage, developed an infection, and received an emergency hysterectomy in Spain. The recovery rate from emergency hysterectomies at the time was astonishingly low; however, Josephine survived. The Free French Government ordered that she be transported to England and to a desk job. She refused her evacuation and remained active in the field until the defeat of the Axis powers in 1945.

After the fall of the fascists, Josephine carried out one last, quite personal mission. She traveled to Buchenwald for what must have been her single most important stage performance. She performed for the rescued death camp prisoners who were still too sick and weak to be moved.

For her long and distinguished service in the war against Nazi tyranny, Josephine was decorated for bravery on three occasions. She received the French Croix de Guerre, the Rosette de la Resistance, and a knighthood from General Charles De Gaulle as a member of the Ordre national de la Légion d'honneur.

After the war, Josephine left her life of espionage behind and returned to the stage. She adopted twelve orphans of Algerian, Korean, Japanese, Finnish, French, Israeli, Moroccan, and Hispanic extraction. She referred to them as her "Rainbow Tribe." By 1947, she had divorced her third husband and married French orchestra leader Jo Bouillon, who helped her raise her children.

Baker returned to America in 1951, and when she was refused service at the Stork Club in Manhattan, Grace Kelly was in attendance and took exception. The future Princess Grace of Monaco took Josephine's arm, and they stormed out together, followed by the rest of Grace's party. Grace Kelly and Josephine became life-long friends, and when Josephine and her large family of orphans faced financial trouble, Princess Grace gave her a palace and financial assistance.

In 1963, Josephine was the only female to speak at the Civil Rights March on Washington, DC. Then, after the assassination of Martin Luther King, she was offered and declined the leadership of King's civil rights organization. She felt that her brood of young children needed her.

Ten years after the March on Washington, Baker opened a show in New York at one of the world's most prestigious venues, Carnegie Hall. Before the first note of the show could be performed, a packed house rose and gave her a standing ovation. The homeless orphan girl from the alleys of St. Louis had finally come home, and America had finally come home to her.

On April 12, 1975, Josephine died of a cerebral hemorrhage. She was the first American woman to receive a military funeral with full honors. Twenty thousand French, Europeans, and Americans who had not forgotten her extraordinary service in the liberation of France joined her funeral procession. Without benefit of athletic prowess, much formal education, gadgetry, military or intelligence training, and armed with little more than her courage and commitment, the homeless girl from the alleys of St. Louis had made an immeasurable difference in the world through her undaunted service to the causes of freedom.

"The things we truly love stay with us always, locked in our hearts as long as life remains." ~ Josephine Baker

IN CONCLUSION

HOLLYWOOD GOES TO GREAT LENGTHS TO CREATE SUPERHEROES AND supervillains, all of whom have some sort of superpower, yet none of them live up to the heroism or down to the depravity of normal human beings. What fictional hero is more awe-inspiring than a one-legged woman crossing the Pyrenees alone in winter to voluntarily return to Nazi-occupied France? What fictional character is more heroic than a homeless child who overcomes abandonment and poverty to become a stage icon, an espionage legend, and a tireless humanitarian? What fictional hero is more inspiring than a man left for dead who comes back to lead the fight for decades more? And what fictional villain is more bone chilling than the smiling, esteemed, hide-and-wait traitor who deliberately plots the deaths of thousands of innocents? At the end of the day, there is no superpower out of Hollywood that can rival the heights and depths of the human heart.

That heart does not change with the transient elements of life. There is greatness all around us, both great good and great evil. Somewhere today, a mother is risking torture and death to save her son and his compatriots. Somewhere today, an overlooked employee is cultivating his image of irrelevance to serve his nation. Somewhere today, a soldier is eating his own bone-grinding pain to throw himself back into the fight. Somewhere today, a patriot is offering her own body in sacrifice to obtain critical information. And somewhere today, a traitor is hurling the decent people of nations onto the turncoat's bonfire of vanity. Everything that mankind has done before, mankind is doing right now. Everything mankind has been before, mankind is today. We only need look to those of the past to understand the possibilities.

But understanding is not the only benefit of parsing out the bits of truth from that abyss of misinformation and deceit we call history. When we see the bravery and determination of that one-legged woman, that homeless child, and that man left for dead, we are inspired to find the same courage, resilience, and tenacity in ourselves. We are called on to rise up to our own potential greatness, because the true human superheroes reveal to us that "we're only human" is not an excuse for failure, but a reason to succeed.

PHOTO GALLERY

Visit our photo gallery with illustrations of some of the individuals and events referenced in this book at our website, BayardandHolmes.com.

TIMELINE IRAN
STONE AGE TO NUCLEAR AGE

WITH THE VOICE OF FORTY-FIVE YEARS IN THE INTELLIGENCE Community, Bayard & Holmes journey through Iran's history to define the challenges that face Western nations today.

A cradle of civilization, Iran has been a political hot spot not just for decades, but for eons. Now, the urgent issue for Western nations is the extent of Iran's nuclear capabilities.

Is Iran developing an atomic bomb? If so, should we do something to stop it? Who is "we," and precisely what would "something" be? How much would "something" cost, and to whom?

This brief, digestible timeline for both amateurs and experts is the perfect start to understanding the dynamics at play in these urgent questions.

Available at BayardandHolmes.com/nonfiction.

ACKNOWLEDGMENTS

Our deepest gratitude to Vicki Hinze, Doug Patteson, and the numerous contacts around the world who provided assistance in the compiling and publishing of this work.

Our humble indebtedness to our families for their tolerance of our late-night conversations and absenteeism to collaborate on this project.

Our abiding thanks to all of the dedicated professionals who gave us their time and efforts in the review and editing process.

Our undying appreciation to our readers. You make our efforts worthwhile.

Thank you, one and all.

DESIGN

———

COVER and LAYOUT
by Piper Bayard

———

Made in the USA
Las Vegas, NV
15 July 2021

26494445R00138